CORIOLANUS

William Shakespeare

Published by the East India Publishing Company
Ottawa, Ontario.

© 2020 East India Publishing Company

Cover Design by EIPC. © 2020
9781774260715

CONTENTS

Act One 7

Act Two 40

Act Three 68

Act Four 99

Act Five 127

Dramatis Personæ

CAIUS MARCIUS CORIOLANUS, a noble Roman

TITUS LARTIUS, General against the Volscians
COMINIUS, General against the Volscians
MENENIUS AGRIPPA, Friend to Coriolanus
SICINIUS VELUTUS, Tribune of the People
JUNIUS BRUTUS, Tribune of the People
YOUNG MARCIUS, son to Coriolanus
A ROMAN HERALD
TULLUS AUFIDIUS, General of the Volscians
LIEUTENANT, to Aufidius
Conspirators with Aufidius
A CITIZEN of Antium
TWO VOLSCIAN GUARDS

VOLUMNIA, Mother to Coriolanus
VIRGILIA, Wife to Coriolanus
VALERIA, Friend to Virgilia
GENTLEWOMAN attending on Virgilia

Roman and Volscian Senators, Patricians, Aediles, Lictors,
Soldiers, Citizens, Messengers, Servants to Aufidius, and
other
Attendants

SCENE: Partly in Rome, and partly in the territories of the
Volscians and Antiates.

ACT I.

[Enter a company of mutinous citizens, with staves, clubs, and
   other weapons.]

FIRST CITIZEN.
   Before we proceed any further, hear me speak.

ALL.
   Speak, speak.

FIRST CITIZEN.
   You are all resolved rather to die than to famish?

ALL.
   Resolved, resolved.

FIRST CITIZEN.
   First, you know Caius Marcius is chief enemy to the people.

ALL.
   We know't, we know't.

FIRST CITIZEN. Let us kill him, and we'll have corn at our own
   price. Is't a verdict?

ALL.
   No more talking on't; let it be done: away, away!

SECOND CITIZEN.
   One word, good citizens.

FIRST CITIZEN. We are accounted poor citizens; the patricians
   good. What authority surfeits on would relieve us; if they
   would yield us but the superfluity, while it were wholesome, we
   might guess they relieved us humanely; but they think we are
   too dear: the leanness that afflicts us, the object of our misery,
   is as an inventory to particularize their abundance; our sufferance is a gain to them.—Let us revenge this with our pikes ere
   we become rakes: for the gods know I speak this in hunger for
   bread, not in thirst for revenge.

SECOND CITIZEN.
Would you proceed especially against Caius Marcius?

FIRST CITIZEN.
Against him first: he's a very dog to the commonalty.

SECOND CITIZEN.
Consider you what services he has done for his country?

FIRST CITIZEN. Very well; and could be content to give him good report for't, but that he pays himself with being proud.

SECOND CITIZEN.
Nay, but speak not maliciously.

FIRST CITIZEN. I say unto you, what he hath done famously he did it to that end: though soft-conscienced men can be content to say it was for his country, he did it to please his mother, and to be partly proud; which he is, even to the altitude of his virtue.

SECOND CITIZEN. What he cannot help in his nature you account a vice in him. You must in no way say he is covetous.

FIRST CITIZEN. If I must not, I need not be barren of accusations; he hath faults, with surplus, to tire in repetition. [Shouts within.] What shouts are these? The other side o' the city is risen: why stay we prating here? to the Capitol!

ALL.
Come, come.

FIRST CITIZEN.
Soft! who comes here?

SECOND CITIZEN.
Worthy Menenius Agrippa; one that hath always loved the people.

FIRST CITIZEN.
He's one honest enough; would all the rest were so!

[Enter MENENIUS AGRIPPA.]

MENENIUS.
  What work's, my countrymen, in hand? where go you
  With bats and clubs? the matter? speak, I pray you.

FIRST CITIZEN. Our business is not unknown to the senate;
  they have had inkling this fortnight what we intend to do,
  which now we'll show 'em in deeds. They say poor suitors
  have strong breaths; they shall know we have strong arms
  too.

MENENIUS.
  Why, masters, my good friends, mine honest neighbours,
  Will you undo yourselves?

FIRST CITIZEN.
  We cannot, sir; we are undone already.

MENENIUS.
  I tell you, friends, most charitable care
  Have the patricians of you. For your wants,
  Your suffering in this dearth, you may as well
  Strike at the heaven with your staves as lift them
  Against the Roman state; whose course will on
  The way it takes, cracking ten thousand curbs
  Of more strong link asunder than can ever
  Appear in your impediment: for the dearth,
  The gods, not the patricians, make it; and
  Your knees to them, not arms, must help. Alack,
  You are transported by calamity
  Thither where more attends you; and you slander
  The helms o' th' state, who care for you like fathers,
  When you curse them as enemies.

FIRST CITIZEN. Care for us! True, indeed! They ne'er
  cared for us yet. Suffer us to famish, and their storehous-
  es crammed with grain; make edicts for usury, to support
  usurers; repeal daily any wholesome act established against
  the rich, and provide more piercing statutes daily to chain
  up and restrain the poor. If the wars eat us not up, they will;
  and there's all the love they bear us.

MENENIUS.
  Either you must
  Confess yourselves wondrous malicious,

Or be accus'd of folly. I shall tell you
A pretty tale: it may be you have heard it;
But, since it serves my purpose, I will venture
To stale't a little more.

FIRST CITIZEN. Well, I'll hear it, sir; yet you must not
think to fob off our disgrace with a tale: but, an't please
you, deliver.

MENENIUS.
There was a time when all the body's members
Rebell'd against the belly; thus accus'd it:—
That only like a gulf it did remain
I' the midst o' the body, idle and unactive,
Still cupboarding the viand, never bearing
Like labour with the rest; where th' other instruments
Did see and hear, devise, instruct, walk, feel,
And, mutually participate, did minister
Unto the appetite and affection common
Of the whole body. The belly answered,—

FIRST CITIZEN.
Well, sir, what answer made the belly?

MENENIUS.
Sir, I shall tell you.—With a kind of smile,
Which ne'er came from the lungs, but even thus,—
For, look you, I may make the belly smile
As well as speak,—it tauntingly replied
To the discontented members, the mutinous parts
That envied his receipt; even so most fitly
As you malign our senators for that
They are not such as you.

FIRST CITIZEN.
Your belly's answer? What!
The kingly crowned head, the vigilant eye,
The counsellor heart, the arm our soldier,
Our steed the leg, the tongue our trumpeter,
With other muniments and petty helps
Is this our fabric, if that they,—

MENENIUS.
    What then?—
    'Fore me, this fellow speaks!—what then? what then?

FIRST CITIZEN.
    Should by the cormorant belly be restrain'd,
    Who is the sink o' the body,—

MENENIUS.
    Well, what then?

FIRST CITIZEN.
    The former agents, if they did complain,
    What could the belly answer?

MENENIUS.
    I will tell you;
    If you'll bestow a small,—of what you have little,—
    Patience awhile, you'll hear the belly's answer.

FIRST CITIZEN.
    You are long about it.

MENENIUS.
    Note me this, good friend;
    Your most grave belly was deliberate,
    Not rash like his accusers, and thus answer'd:
    'True is it, my incorporate friends,' quoth he,
    'That I receive the general food at first
    Which you do live upon; and fit it is,
    Because I am the storehouse and the shop
    Of the whole body: but, if you do remember,
    I send it through the rivers of your blood,
    Even to the court, the heart,—to the seat o' the brain;
    And, through the cranks and offices of man,
    The strongest nerves and small inferior veins
    From me receive that natural competency
    Whereby they live: and though that all at once
    You, my good friends,'—this says the belly,—mark me,—

FIRST CITIZEN.
    Ay, sir; well, well.

MENENIUS.

William Shakespeare

'Though all at once cannot
See what I do deliver out to each,
Yet I can make my audit up, that all
From me do back receive the flour of all,
And leave me but the bran.' What say you to't?

FIRST CITIZEN.
It was an answer: how apply you this?

MENENIUS.
The senators of Rome are this good belly,
And you the mutinous members; for, examine
Their counsels and their cares; digest things rightly
Touching the weal o' the common; you shall find
No public benefit which you receive
But it proceeds or comes from them to you,
And no way from yourselves.—What do you think,
You, the great toe of this assembly?

FIRST CITIZEN.
I the great toe? why the great toe?

MENENIUS.
For that, being one o' the lowest, basest, poorest,
Of this most wise rebellion, thou go'st foremost:
Thou rascal, that art worst in blood to run,
Lead'st first to win some vantage.—
But make you ready your stiff bats and clubs:
Rome and her rats are at the point of battle;
The one side must have bale.—

[Enter CAIUS MARCIUS.]

Hail, noble Marcius!

MARCIUS.
Thanks.—What's the matter, you dissentious rogues
That, rubbing the poor itch of your opinion,
Make yourselves scabs?

FIRST CITIZEN.
We have ever your good word.

MARCIUS.

  He that will give good words to thee will flatter
  Beneath abhorring.—What would you have, you curs,
  That like nor peace nor war? The one affrights you,
  The other makes you proud. He that trusts to you,
  Where he should find you lions, finds you hares;
  Where foxes, geese: you are no surer, no,
  Than is the coal of fire upon the ic,
  Or hailstone in the sun. Your virtue is
  To make him worthy whose offence subdues him,
  And curse that justice did it. Who deserves greatness
  Deserves your hate; and your affections are
  A sick man's appetite, who desires most that
  Which would increase his evil. He that depends
  Upon your favours swims with fins of lead,
  And hews down oaks with rushes. Hang ye! Trust ye!
  With every minute you do change a mind;
  And call him noble that was now your hate,
  Him vile that was your garland. What's the matter,
  That in these several places of the city
  You cry against the noble senate, who,
  Under the gods, keep you in awe, which else
  Would feed on one another?—What's their seeking?

MENENIUS.

  For corn at their own rates; whereof they say
  The city is well stor'd.

MARCIUS.

  Hang 'em! They say!
  They'll sit by th' fire and presume to know
  What's done i' the Capitol; who's like to rise,
  Who thrives and who declines; side factions, and give out
  Conjectural marriages; making parties strong,
  And feebling such as stand not in their liking
  Below their cobbled shoes. They say there's grain enough!
  Would the nobility lay aside their ruth
  And let me use my sword, I'd make a quarry
  With thousands of these quarter'd slaves, as high
  As I could pick my lance.

MENENIUS.
  Nay, these are almost thoroughly persuaded;
  For though abundantly they lack discretion,
  Yet are they passing cowardly. But, I beseech you,
  What says the other troop?

MARCIUS.
  They are dissolved: hang 'em!
  They said they were an-hungry; sigh'd forth proverbs,—
  That hunger broke stone walls, that dogs must eat,
  That meat was made for mouths, that the gods sent not
  Corn for the rich men only:—with these shreds
  They vented their complainings; which being answer'd,
  And a petition granted them,—a strange one,
  To break the heart of generosity,
  And make bold power look pale,—they threw their caps
  As they would hang them on the horns o' the moon,
  Shouting their emulation.

MENENIUS.
  What is granted them?

MARCIUS.
  Five tribunes, to defend their vulgar wisdoms,
  Of their own choice: one's Junius Brutus,
  Sicinius Velutus, and I know not.—'Sdeath!
  The rabble should have first unroof'd the city
  Ere so prevail'd with me: it will in time
  Win upon power, and throw forth greater themes
  For insurrection's arguing.

MENENIUS.
  This is strange.

MARCIUS.
  Go get you home, you fragments!

[Enter a MESSENGER, hastily.]

MESSENGER.
  Where's Caius Marcius?

MARCIUS.
  Here: what's the matter?

MESSENGER.
The news is, sir, the Volsces are in arms.

MARCIUS.
I am glad on't: then we shall ha' means to vent
Our musty superfluity.—See, our best elders.

[Enter COMINIUS, TITUS LARTIUS, and other SENA-
TORS; JUNIUS BRUTUS and SICINIUS VELUTUS.]

FIRST SENATOR.
Marcius, 'tis true that you have lately told us:—
The Volsces are in arms.

MARCIUS.
They have a leader,
Tullus Aufidius, that will put you to't.
I sin in envying his nobility;
And were I anything but what I am,
I would wish me only he.

COMINIUS.
You have fought together.

MARCIUS.
Were half to half the world by the ears, and he
Upon my party, I'd revolt, to make
Only my wars with him: he is a lion
That I am proud to hunt.

FIRST SENATOR.
Then, worthy Marcius,
Attend upon Cominius to these wars.

COMINIUS.
It is your former promise.

MARCIUS.
Sir, it is;
And I am constant.—Titus Lartius, thou
Shalt see me once more strike at Tullus' face.
What, art thou stiff? stand'st out?

TITUS LARTIUS.
  No, Caius Marcius;
  I'll lean upon one crutch and fight with the other
  Ere stay behind this business.

MENENIUS.
  O, true bred!

FIRST SENATOR.
  Your company to the Capitol; where, I know,
  Our greatest friends attend us.

TITUS LARTIUS.
  Lead you on.
  Follow, Cominius; we must follow you;
  Right worthy your priority.

COMINIUS.
  Noble Marcius!

FIRST SENATOR.
  Hence to your homes; be gone!
  [To the Citizens.]

MARCIUS.
  Nay, let them follow:
  The Volsces have much corn; take these rats thither
  To gnaw their garners.—Worshipful mutineers,
  Your valour puts well forth: pray follow.

[Exeunt Senators, COM., MAR, TIT., and MENEN. Citizens
  steal away.]

SICINIUS.
  Was ever man so proud as is this Marcius?

BRUTUS.
  He has no equal.

SICINIUS.
  When we were chosen tribunes for the people,—

BRUTUS.
  Mark'd you his lip and eyes?

SICINIUS.
  Nay, but his taunts!

BRUTUS.
  Being mov'd, he will not spare to gird the gods.

SICINIUS.
  Bemock the modest moon.

BRUTUS.
  The present wars devour him: he is grown
  Too proud to be so valiant.

SICINIUS.
  Such a nature,
  Tickled with good success, disdains the shadow
  Which he treads on at noon: but I do wonder
  His insolence can brook to be commanded
  Under Cominius.

BRUTUS.
  Fame, at the which he aims,—
  In whom already he is well grac'd,—cannot
  Better be held, nor more attain'd, than by
  A place below the first: for what miscarries
  Shall be the general's fault, though he perform
  To th' utmost of a man; and giddy censure
  Will then cry out of Marcius 'O, if he
  Had borne the business!'

SICINIUS.
  Besides, if things go well,
  Opinion, that so sticks on Marcius, shall
  Of his demerits rob Cominius.

BRUTUS.
  Come:
  Half all Cominius' honours are to Marcius,
  Though Marcius earn'd them not; and all his faults
  To Marcius shall be honours, though, indeed,
  In aught he merit not.

SICINIUS.
  Let's hence and hear
  How the dispatch is made; and in what fashion,
  More than in singularity, he goes
  Upon this present action.

BRUTUS.
  Let's along.

[Exeunt.]

SCENE II. CORIOLI. THE SENATE HOUSE.

[Enter TULLUS AUFIDIUS and certain SENATORS.]

FIRST SENATOR.
  So, your opinion is, Aufidius,
  That they of Rome are enter'd in our counsels
  And know how we proceed.

AUFIDIUS.
  Is it not yours?
  What ever have been thought on in this state,
  That could be brought to bodily act ere Rome
  Had circumvention! 'Tis not four days gone
  Since I heard thence; these are the words: I think
  I have the letter here;yes, here it is:
  [Reads.]
  'They have pressed a power, but it is not known
  Whether for east or west: the dearth is great;
  The people mutinous: and it is rumour'd,
  Cominius, Marcius your old enemy,—
  Who is of Rome worse hated than of you,—
  And Titus Lartius, a most valiant Roman,
  These three lead on this preparation
  Whither 'tis bent: most likely 'tis for you:
  Consider of it.'

FIRST SENATOR.
  Our army's in the field:
  We never yet made doubt but Rome was ready
  To answer us.

AUFIDIUS.
  Nor did you think it folly
  To keep your great pretences veil'd till when
  They needs must show themselves; which in the hatching,
  It seem'd, appear'd to Rome. By the discovery
  We shall be shorten'd in our aim; which was,
  To take in many towns ere, almost, Rome
  Should know we were afoot.

SECOND SENATOR.
  Noble Aufidius,
  Take your commission; hie you to your bands;
  Let us alone to guard Corioli:
  If they set down before's, for the remove
  Bring up your army; but I think you'll find
  They've not prepared for us.

AUFIDIUS.
  O, doubt not that;
  I speak from certainties. Nay, more,
  Some parcels of their power are forth already,
  And only hitherward. I leave your honours.
  If we and Caius Marcius chance to meet,
  'Tis sworn between us we shall ever strike
  Till one can do no more.

ALL.
  The gods assist you!

AUFIDIUS.
  And keep your honours safe!

FIRST SENATOR.
  Farewell.

SECOND SENATOR.
  Farewell.

ALL. Farewell.

[Exeunt.]

SCENE III. ROME. AN APARTMNET IN MARCIUS' HOUSE.

[Enter VOLUMNIA and VIRGILIA; they sit down on two low stools and sew.]

VOLUMNIA. I pray you, daughter, sing, or express yourself in a more comfortable sort; if my son were my husband, I should freelier rejoice in that absence wherein he won honour than in the embracements of his bed where he would show most love. When yet he was but tender-bodied, and the only son of my womb; when youth with comeliness pluck'd all gaze his way; when, for a day of kings' entreaties, a mother should not sell him an hour from her beholding; I,—considering how honour would become such a person; that it was no better than picture-like to hang by th' wall if renown made it not stir;—was pleased to let him seek danger where he was to find fame. To a cruel war I sent him; from whence he returned his brows bound with oak. I tell thee, daughter, I sprang not more in joy at first hearing he was a man-child than now in first seeing he had proved himself a man.

VIRGILIA.
But had he died in the business, madam? how then?

VOLUMNIA. Then his good report should have been my son; I therein would have found issue. Hear me profess sincerely,—had I a dozen sons, each in my love alike, and none less dear than thine and my good Marcius, I had rather had eleven die nobly for their country than one voluptuously surfeit out of action.

[Enter a GENTLEWOMAN.]

GENTLEWOMAN.
Madam, the Lady Valeria is come to visit you.

VIRGILIA.
Beseech you, give me leave to retire myself.

VOLUMNIA.
Indeed you shall not.
Methinks I hear hither your husband's drum;
See him pluck Aufidius down by the hair;

As children from a bear, the Volsces shunning him:
Methinks I see him stamp thus, and call thus:—
'Come on, you cowards! you were got in fear
Though you were born in Rome:' his bloody brow
With his mail'd hand then wiping, forth he goes,
Like to a harvest-man that's tasked to mow
Or all, or lose his hire.

VIRGILIA.
His bloody brow! O Jupiter, no blood!

VOLUMNIA.
Away, you fool! It more becomes a man
Than gilt his trophy: the breasts of Hecuba,
When she did suckle Hector, looked not lovelier
Than Hector's forehead when it spit forth blood
At Grecian swords contending.—Tell Valeria
We are fit to bid her welcome.

[Exit GENTLEWOMAN.]

VIRGILIA.
Heavens bless my lord from fell Aufidius!

VOLUMNIA.
He'll beat Aufidius' head below his knee,
And tread upon his neck.

[Re-enter GENTLEWOMAN, with VALERIA and her Usher.]

VALERIA.
My ladies both, good-day to you.

VOLUMNIA.
Sweet madam.

VIRGILIA.
I am glad to see your ladyship.

VALERIA. How do you both? you are manifest house-keepers. What are you sewing here? A fine spot, in good faith.—How does your little son?

VIRGILIA.
I thank your ladyship; well, good madam.

VOLUMNIA. He had rather see the swords and hear a drum than look upon his schoolmaster.

VALERIA. O' my word, the father's son: I'll swear 'tis a very pretty boy. O' my troth, I looked upon him o' Wednesday, half an hour together: has such a confirmed countenance. I saw him run after a gilded butterfly; and when he caught it he let it go again; and after it again; and over and over he comes, and up again; catched it again; or whether his fall enraged him, or how 'twas, he did so set his teeth and tear it; O, I warrant, how he mammocked it!

VOLUMNIA.
One on's father's moods.

VALERIA.
Indeed, la, 'tis a noble child.

VIRGILIA.
A crack, madam.

VALERIA. Come, lay aside your stitchery; I must have you play the idle huswife with me this afternoon.

VIRGILIA.
No, good madam; I will not out of doors.

VALERIA.
Not out of doors!

VOLUMNIA.
She shall, she shall.

VIRGILIA. Indeed, no, by your patience; I'll not over the threshold till my lord return from the wars.

VALERIA. Fie, you confine yourself most unreasonably; come, you must go visit the good lady that lies in.

VIRGILIA. I will wish her speedy strength, and visit her with my prayers; but I cannot go thither.

VOLUMNIA.
Why, I pray you?

VIRGILIA.
'Tis not to save labour, nor that I want love.

VALERIA. You would be another Penelope; yet they say all
the yarn she spun in Ulysses' absence did but fill Ithaca
full of moths. Come; I would your cambric were sensible
as your finger, that you might leave pricking it for pity.—
Come, you shall go with us.

VIRGILIA.
No, good madam, pardon me; indeed I will not forth.

VALERIA. In truth, la, go with me; and I'll tell you excellent
news of your husband.

VIRGILIA.
O, good madam, there can be none yet.

VALERIA. Verily, I do not jest with you; there came news
from him last night.

VIRGILIA.
Indeed, madam?

VALERIA. In earnest, it's true; I heard a senator speak it.
Thus it is:—the Volsces have an army forth; against whom
Cominius the general is gone, with one part of our Roman
power: your lord and Titus Lartius are set down before
their city Corioli; they nothing doubt prevailing, and to
make it brief wars. This is true, on mine honour; and so, I
pray, go with us.

VIRGILIA. Give me excuse, good madam; I will obey you
in everything hereafter.

VOLUMNIA. Let her alone, lady; as she is now, she will but
disease our better mirth.

VALERIA. In troth, I think she would.—Fare you well,
then.—Come, good sweet lady.—Pr'ythee, Virgilia, turn
thy solemness out o' door and go along with us.

VIRGILIA.
  No, at a word, madam; indeed I must not. I wish you much
  mirth.

VALERIA.
  Well then, farewell.

[Exeunt.]

SCENE IV. BEFORE CORIOLI.

[Enter, with drum and colours, MARCIUS, TITUS LARTI-
  US, Officers, and soldiers.]

MARCIUS.
  Yonder comes news:—a wager they have met.

LARTIUS.
  My horse to yours, no.

MARCIUS.
  'Tis done.

LARTIUS.
  Agreed.

[Enter a Messenger.]

MARCIUS.
  Say, has our general met the enemy?

MESSENGER.
  They lie in view; but have not spoke as yet.

LARTIUS.
  So, the good horse is mine.

MARCIUS.
  I'll buy him of you.

LARTIUS.
  No, I'll nor sell nor give him: lend you him I will
  For half a hundred years.—Summon the town.

MARCIUS.
  How far off lie these armies?

MESSENGER.
  Within this mile and half.

MARCIUS.
  Then shall we hear their 'larum, and they ours.—
  Now, Mars, I pr'ythee, make us quick in work,
  That we with smoking swords may march from hence
  To help our fielded friends!—Come, blow thy blast.

[They sound a parley. Enter, on the Walls, some Senators and
  others.]

Tullus Aufidius, is he within your walls?

FIRST SENATOR.
  No, nor a man that fears you less than he,
  That's lesser than a little.
  [Drum afar off]
  Hark, our drums
  Are bringing forth our youth! we'll break our walls
  Rather than they shall pound us up: our gates,
  Which yet seem shut, we have but pinn'd with rushes;
  They'll open of themselves.
  [Alarum far off.]
  Hark you far off!
  There is Aufidius; list what work he makes
  Amongst your cloven army.

MARCIUS.
  O, they are at it!

LARTIUS.
  Their noise be our instruction.—Ladders, ho!

[The Volsces enter and pass over.]

MARCIUS.
  They fear us not, but issue forth their city.
  Now put your shields before your hearts, and fight
  With hearts more proof than shields.—Advance, brave
  Titus:
  They do disdain us much beyond our thoughts,
  Which makes me sweat with wrath.—Come on, my fel-
  lows:

He that retires, I'll take him for a Volsce,
And he shall feel mine edge.

[Alarums, and exeunt Romeans and Volsces fighting. Romans are beaten back to their trenches. Re-enter MARCIUS.]

MARCIUS.
All the contagion of the south light on you,
You shames of Rome!—you herd of—Boils and plagues
Plaster you o'er, that you may be abhorr'd
Farther than seen, and one infect another
Against the wind a mile! You souls of geese
That bear the shapes of men, how have you run
From slaves that apes would beat! Pluto and hell!
All hurt behind; backs red, and faces pale
With flight and agued fear! Mend, and charge home,
Or, by the fires of heaven, I'll leave the foe
And make my wars on you: look to't: come on;
If you'll stand fast we'll beat them to their wives,
As they us to our trenches.

[Another alarum. The Volsces and Romans re-enter, and the fight is renewed. The Volsces retire into Corioli, and MARCIUS follows them to the gates.]

So, now the gates are ope:—now prove good seconds:
'Tis for the followers fortune widens them,
Not for the fliers: mark me, and do the like.

[He enters the gates]

FIRST SOLDIER.
Fool-hardiness: not I.

SECOND SOLDIER.
Nor I.

[MARCIUS is shut in.]

FIRST SOLDIER.
See, they have shut him in.

ALL.
To th' pot, I warrant him.

[Alarum continues]

[Re-enter TITUS LARTIUS.]

LARTIUS.
  What is become of Marcius?

ALL.
  Slain, sir, doubtless.

FIRST SOLDIER.
  Following the fliers at the very heels,
  With them he enters; who, upon the sudden,
  Clapp'd-to their gates: he is himself alone,
  To answer all the city.

LARTIUS.
  O noble fellow!
  Who sensible, outdares his senseless sword,
  And when it bows stands up! Thou art left, Marcius:
  A carbuncle entire, as big as thou art,
  Were not so rich a jewel. Thou wast a soldier
  Even to Cato's wish, not fierce and terrible
  Only in strokes; but with thy grim looks and
  The thunder-like percussion of thy sounds
  Thou mad'st thine enemies shake, as if the world
  Were feverous and did tremble.

[Re-enter MARCIUS, bleeding, assaulted by the enemy.]

FIRST SOLDIER.
  Look, sir.

LARTIUS.
  O, 'tis Marcius!
  Let's fetch him off, or make remain alike.

[They fight, and all enter the city.]

SCENE V. WITHIN CORIOLI. A STREET.

[Enter certain Romans, with spoils.]

FIRST ROMAN.
  This will I carry to Rome.

SECOND ROMAN.
  And I this.

THIRD ROMAN.
  A murrain on't! I took this for silver.

[Alarum continues still afar off.]

[Enter MARCIUS and TITUS LARTIUS with a trumpet.]

MARCIUS.
  See here these movers that do prize their hours
  At a crack'd drachma! Cushions, leaden spoons,
  Irons of a doit, doublets that hangmen would
  Bury with those that wore them, these base slaves,
  Ere yet the fight be done, pack up:—down with them!—
  And hark, what noise the general makes!—To him!—
  There is the man of my soul's hate, Aufidius,
  Piercing our Romans; then, valiant Titus, take
  Convenient numbers to make good the city;
  Whilst I, with those that have the spirit, will haste
  To help Cominius.

LARTIUS.
  Worthy sir, thou bleed'st;
  Thy exercise hath been too violent
  For a second course of fight.

MARCIUS.
  Sir, praise me not;
  My work hath yet not warm'd me: fare you well;
  The blood I drop is rather physical
  Than dangerous to me: to Aufidius thus
  I will appear, and fight.

LARTIUS.
  Now the fair goddess, Fortune,
  Fall deep in love with thee; and her great charms
  Misguide thy opposers' swords! Bold gentleman,
  Prosperity be thy page!

MARCIUS.
  Thy friend no less
  Than those she placeth highest!—So farewell.

LARTIUS.
  Thou worthiest Marcius!—

[Exit MARCIUS.]

Go, sound thy trumpet in the market-place;
  Call thither all the officers o' the town,
  Where they shall know our mind: away!

[Exeunt.]

SCENE VI. NEAR THE CAMP OF COMINIUS.

[Enter COMINIUS and Foreces, retreating.]

COMINIUS.
  Breathe you, my friends: well fought; we are come off
  Like Romans, neither foolish in our stands
  Nor cowardly in retire: believe me, sirs,
  We shall be charg'd again. Whiles we have struck,
  By interims and conveying gusts we have heard
  The charges of our friends. The Roman gods,
  Lead their successes as we wish our own,
  That both our powers, with smiling fronts encountering,
  May give you thankful sacrifice!—

[Enter A MESSENGER.]

Thy news?

MESSENGER.
  The citizens of Corioli have issued,
  And given to Lartius and to Marcius battle:
  I saw our party to their trenches driven,
  And then I came away.

COMINIUS.
  Though thou speak'st truth,
  Methinks thou speak'st not well. How long is't since?

MESSENGER.
  Above an hour, my lord.

COMINIUS.
  'Tis not a mile; briefly we heard their drums:
  How couldst thou in a mile confound an hour,
  And bring thy news so late?

MESSENGER.
  Spies of the Volsces
  Held me in chase, that I was forc'd to wheel
  Three or four miles about; else had I, sir,
  Half an hour since brought my report.

COMINIUS.
  Who's yonder,
  That does appear as he were flay'd? O gods!
  He has the stamp of Marcius; and I have
  Before-time seen him thus.

MARCIUS.
  [Within.] Come I too late?

COMINIUS.
  The shepherd knows not thunder from a tabor
  More than I know the sound of Marcius' tongue
  From every meaner man.

[Enter MARCIUS.]

MARCIUS.
  Come I too late?

COMINIUS.
  Ay, if you come not in the blood of others,
  But mantled in your own.

MARCIUS.
  O! let me clip ye
  In arms as sound as when I woo'd; in heart
  As merry as when our nuptial day was done,
  And tapers burn'd to bedward.

COMINIUS.
  Flower of warriors,
  How is't with Titus Lartius?

MARCIUS.
  As with a man busied about decrees:
  Condemning some to death and some to exile;
  Ransoming him or pitying, threat'ning the other;
  Holding Corioli in the name of Rome,
  Even like a fawning greyhound in the leash,
  To let him slip at will.

COMINIUS.
  Where is that slave
  Which told me they had beat you to your trenches?
  Where's he? call him hither.

MARCIUS.
  Let him alone;
  He did inform the truth: but for our gentlemen,
  The common file,—a plague!—tribunes for them!—
  The mouse ne'er shunned the cat as they did budge
  From rascals worse than they.

COMINIUS.
  But how prevail'd you?

MARCIUS.
  Will the time serve to tell? I do not think.
  Where is the enemy? are you lords o' the field?
  If not, why cease you till you are so?

COMINIUS.
  Marcius,
  We have at disadvantage fought, and did
  Retire, to win our purpose.

MARCIUS.
  How lies their battle? know you on which side
  They have placed their men of trust?

COMINIUS.
  As I guess, Marcius,
  Their bands in the vaward are the Antiates,
  Of their best trust; o'er them Aufidius,
  Their very heart of hope.

MARCIUS.
I do beseech you,
By all the battles wherein we have fought,
By the blood we have shed together, by the vows
We have made to endure friends, that you directly
Set me against Aufidius and his Antiates;
And that you not delay the present, but,
Filling the air with swords advanc'd and darts,
We prove this very hour.

COMINIUS.
Though I could wish
You were conducted to a gentle bath,
And balms applied to you, yet dare I never
Deny your asking: take your choice of those
That best can aid your action.

MARCIUS.
Those are they
That most are willing.—If any such be here,—
As it were sin to doubt,—that love this painting
Wherein you see me smear'd; if any fear
Lesser his person than an ill report;
If any think brave death outweighs bad life,
And that his country's dearer than himself;
Let him alone, or so many so minded,
Wave thus [waving his hand], to express his disposition,
And follow Marcius.

[They all shout and wave their swords; take him up in their
arms and cast up their caps.]

O, me alone! Make you a sword of me?
If these shows be not outward, which of you
But is four Volsces? none of you but is
Able to bear against the great Aufidius
A shield as hard as his. A certain number,
Though thanks to all, must I select from all: the rest
Shall bear the business in some other fight,
As cause will be obey'd. Please you to march;
And four shall quickly draw out my command,
Which men are best inclin'd.

COMINIUS.
  March on, my fellows;
  Make good this ostentation, and you shall
  Divide in all with us.

[Exeunt.]

SCENE VII. THE GATES OF CORIOLI.

[TITUS LARTIUS, having set a guard upon Corioli, going
  with drum and trumpet toward COMINIUS and CAIUS
  MARCIUS, enters with a LIEUTENANT, a party of Soldiers, and a Scout.]

LARTIUS.
  So, let the ports be guarded: keep your duties
  As I have set them down. If I do send, despatch
  Those centuries to our aid; the rest will serve
  For a short holding: if we lose the field
  We cannot keep the town.

LIEUTENANT.
  Fear not our care, sir.

LARTIUS.
  Hence, and shut your gates upon's.—
  Our guider, come; to the Roman camp conduct us.

[Exeunt.]

SCENE VIII. A FIELD OF BATTLE BETWEEN THE ROMAN AND THE VOLSCIAN CAMPS.

[Alarum. Enter, from opposite sides, MARCIUS and AU-
  FIDIUS.]

MARCIUS.
  I'll fight with none but thee, for I do hate thee
  Worse than a promise-breaker.

AUFIDIUS.
  We hate alike:
  Not Afric owns a serpent I abhor
  More than thy fame and envy. Fix thy foot.

MARCIUS.
  Let the first budger die the other's slave,
  And the gods doom him after!

AUFIDIUS.
  If I fly, Marcius,
  Halloo me like a hare.

MARCIUS.
  Within these three hours, Tullus,
  Alone I fought in your Corioli walls,
  And made what work I pleas'd: 'tis not my blood
  Wherein thou seest me mask'd: for thy revenge
  Wrench up thy power to the highest.

AUFIDIUS.
  Wert thou the Hector
  That was the whip of your bragg'd progeny,
  Thou shouldst not scape me here.—

[They fight, and certain Volsces come to the aid of AUFIDI-
  US.]

Officious, and not valiant,—you have sham'd me
  In your condemned seconds.

[Exeunt fighting, driven in by MAR.]

SCENE IX. THE ROMAN CAMP.

[Alarum. A retreat is sounded. Flourish. Enter, at one side,
  COMINIUS and Romans; at the other side, MARCIUS,
  with his arm in a scarf, and other Romans.]

COMINIUS.
  If I should tell thee o'er this thy day's work,
  Thou't not believe thy deeds: but I'll report it
  Where senators shall mingle tears with smiles;
  Where great patricians shall attend, and shrug,
  I' the end admire; where ladies shall be frighted
  And, gladly quak'd, hear more; where the dull tribunes,
  That, with the fusty plebeians, hate thine honours,
  Shall say, against their hearts 'We thank the gods
  Our Rome hath such a soldier.'

Yet cam'st thou to a morsel of this feast,
Having fully dined before.

[Enter TITUS LARTIUS, with his power, from the pursuit.]

LARTIUS.
  O general,
  Here is the steed, we the caparison:
  Hadst thou beheld,—

MARCIUS.
  Pray now, no more: my mother,
  Who has a charter to extol her blood,
  When she does praise me grieves me. I have done
  As you have done,—that's what I can; induced
  As you have been,—that's for my country:
  He that has but effected his good will
  Hath overta'en mine act.

COMINIUS.
  You shall not be
  The grave of your deserving; Rome must know
  The value of her own: 'twere a concealment
  Worse than a theft, no less than a traducement,
  To hide your doings; and to silence that
  Which, to the spire and top of praises vouch'd,
  Would seem but modest: therefore, I beseech you,—
  In sign of what you are, not to reward
  What you have done,—before our army hear me.

MARCIUS.
  I have some wounds upon me, and they smart
  To hear themselves remember'd.

COMINIUS.
  Should they not,
  Well might they fester 'gainst ingratitude,
  And tent themselves with death. Of all the horses,—
  Whereof we have ta'en good, and good store,—of all
  The treasure in this field achiev'd and city,
  We render you the tenth; to be ta'en forth
  Before the common distribution at
  Your only choice.

MARCIUS.
  I thank you, general,
  But cannot make my heart consent to take
  A bribe to pay my sword: I do refuse it;
  And stand upon my common part with those
  That have beheld the doing.

[A long flourish. They all cry 'Marcius, Marcius!', cast up
  their
  caps and lances. COMINIUS and LARTIUS stand bare.]

May these same instruments which you profane
  Never sound more! When drums and trumpets shall
  I' the field prove flatterers, let courts and cities be
  Made all of false-fac'd soothing.
  When steel grows soft as the parasite's silk,
  Let him be made a coverture for the wars.
  No more, I say! for that I have not wash'd
  My nose that bled, or foil'd some debile wretch,—
  Which, without note, here's many else have done,—
  You shout me forth in acclamations hyperbolical;
  As if I loved my little should be dieted
  In praises sauc'd with lies.

COMINIUS.
  Too modest are you;
  More cruel to your good report than grateful
  To us that give you truly; by your patience,
  If 'gainst yourself you be incens'd, we'll put you,—
  Like one that means his proper harm,—in manacles,
  Then reason safely with you.—Therefore be it known,
  As to us, to all the world, that Caius Marcius
  Wears this war's garland: in token of the which,
  My noble steed, known to the camp, I give him,
  With all his trim belonging; and from this time,
  For what he did before Corioli, call him,
  With all the applause—and clamour of the host,
  'Caius Marcius Coriolanus.'—
  Bear the addition nobly ever!

[Flourish. Trumpets sound, and drums]

ALL.
Caius Marcius Coriolanus!

CORIOLANUS.
I will go wash;
And when my face is fair you shall perceive
Whether I blush or no: howbeit, I thank you;—
I mean to stride your steed; and at all times
To undercrest your good addition
To the fairness of my power.

COMINIUS.
So, to our tent;
Where, ere we do repose us, we will write
To Rome of our success.—You, Titus Lartius,
Must to Corioli back: send us to Rome
The best, with whom we may articulate
For their own good and ours.

LARTIUS.
I shall, my lord.

CORIOLANUS.
The gods begin to mock me. I, that now
Refus'd most princely gifts, am bound to beg
Of my lord general.

COMINIUS.
Take't: 'tis yours.—What is't?

CORIOLANUS.
I sometime lay here in Corioli
At a poor man's house; he used me kindly:
He cried to me; I saw him prisoner;
But then Aufidius was within my view,
And wrath o'erwhelmed my pity: I request you
To give my poor host freedom.

COMINIUS.
O, well begg'd!
Were he the butcher of my son, he should
Be free as is the wind. Deliver him, Titus.

LARTIUS.
  Marcius, his name?

CORIOLANUS.
  By Jupiter, forgot:—
  I am weary; yea, my memory is tir'd.—
  Have we no wine here?

COMINIUS.
  Go we to our tent:
  The blood upon your visage dries; 'tis time
  It should be look'd to: come.

[Exeunt.]

SCENE X. THE CAMP OF THE VOLSCES.

[A flourish. Cornets. Enter TULLUS AUFIDIUS, bloody,
  with two or three soldiers.]

AUFIDIUS.
  The town is ta'en.

FIRST SOLDIER.
  'Twill be delivered back on good condition.

AUFIDIUS.
  Condition!
  I would I were a Roman; for I cannot,
  Being a Volsce, be that I am.—Condition?
  What good condition can a treaty find
  I' the part that is at mercy?—Five times, Marcius,
  I have fought with thee; so often hast thou beat me;
  And wouldst do so, I think, should we encounter
  As often as we eat.—By the elements,
  If e'er again I meet him beard to beard,
  He's mine or I am his: mine emulation
  Hath not that honour in't it had; for where
  I thought to crush him in an equal force,—
  True sword to sword,—I'll potch at him some way,
  Or wrath or craft may get him.

FIRST SOLDIER.
  He's the devil.

AUFIDIUS.
  Bolder, though not so subtle. My valour's poisoned
  With only suffering stain by him; for him
  Shall fly out of itself: nor sleep nor sanctuary,
  Being naked, sick; nor fane nor Capitol,
  The prayers of priests nor times of sacrifice,
  Embarquements all of fury, shall lift up
  Their rotten privilege and custom 'gainst
  My hate to Marcius: where I find him, were it
  At home, upon my brother's guard, even there,
  Against the hospitable canon, would I
  Wash my fierce hand in's heart. Go you to the city;
  Learn how 'tis held; and what they are that must
  Be hostages for Rome.

FIRST SOLDIER.
  Will not you go?

AUFIDIUS.
  I am attended at the cypress grove: I pray you,—
  'Tis south the city mills,—bring me word thither
  How the world goes, that to the pace of it
  I may spur on my journey.

FIRST SOLDIER.
  I shall, sir.

[Exeunt.]

ACT II.

[Enter MENENIUS, SICINIUS, and BRUTUS.]

MENENIUS.
  The augurer tells me we shall have news tonight.

BRUTUS.
  Good or bad?

MENENIUS.
  Not according to the prayer of the people, for they love not
  Marcius.

SICINIUS.
  Nature teaches beasts to know their friends.

MENENIUS.
  Pray you, who does the wolf love?

SICINIUS.
  The lamb.

MENENIUS.
  Ay, to devour him, as the hungry plebeians would the noble
  Marcius.

BRUTUS.
  He's a lamb indeed, that baas like a bear.

MENENIUS. He's a bear indeed, that lives like a lamb. You
  two are old men: tell me one thing that I shall ask you.

BOTH TRIBUNES.
  Well, sir.

MENENIUS. In what enormity is Marcius poor in, that you
  two have not in abundance?

BRUTUS.
  He's poor in no one fault, but stored with all.

SICINIUS.
  Especially in pride.

BRUTUS.
  And topping all others in boasting.

MENENIUS. This is strange now: do you two know how
  you are censured here in the city, I mean of us o' the right-
  hand file? Do you?

BOTH TRIBUNES.
  Why, how are we censured?

MENENIUS.
  Because you talk of pride now,—will you not be angry?

BOTH TRIBUNES.
  Well, well, sir, well.

MENENIUS. Why, 'tis no great matter; for a very little thief
  of occasion will rob you of a great deal of patience: give
  your dispositions the reins, and be angry at your pleasures;
  at the least, if you take it as a pleasure to you in being so.
  You blame Marcius for being proud?

BRUTUS.
  We do it not alone, sir.

MENENIUS. I know you can do very little alone; for your
  helps are many, or else your actions would grow wondrous
  single: your abilities are too infant-like for doing much
  alone. You talk of pride: O that you could turn your eyes
  toward the napes of your necks, and make but an interior
  survey of your good selves! O that you could!

BOTH TRIBUNES.
  What then, sir?

MENENIUS. Why, then you should discover a brace of un-
  meriting, proud, violent, testy magistrates,—alias fools,—
  as any in Rome.

SICINIUS.
  Menenius, you are known well enough too.

MENENIUS. I am known to be a humorous patrician, and one that loves a cup of hot wine with not a drop of allaying Tiber in't; said to be something imperfect in favouring the first complaint, hasty and tinder-like upon too trivial motion; one that converses more with the buttock of the night than with the forehead of the morning. What I think I utter, and spend my malice in my breath. Meeting two such wealsmen as you are,—I cannot call you Lycurguses,—if the drink you give me touch my palate adversely, I make a crooked face at it. I cannot say your worships have delivered the matter well when I find the ass in compound with the major part of your syllables; and though I must be content to bear with those that say you are reverend grave men, yet they lie deadly that tell you have good faces. If you see this in the map of my microcosm, follows it that I am known well enough too? What harm can your bisson conspectuities glean out of this character, if I be known well enough too?

BRUTUS.
Come, sir, come, we know you well enough.

MENENIUS. You know neither me, yourselves, nor anything. You are ambitious for poor knaves' caps and legs; you wear out a good wholesome forenoon in hearing a cause between an orange-wife and a fosset-seller, and then rejourn the controversy of threepence to a second day of audience.—When you are hearing a matter between party and party, if you chance to be pinched with the colic, you make faces like mummers, set up the bloody flag against all patience, and, in roaring for a chamber-pot, dismiss the controversy bleeding, the more entangled by your hearing: all the peace you make in their cause is calling both the parties knaves. You are a pair of strange ones.

BRUTUS. Come, come, you are well understood to be a perfecter giber for the table than a necessary bencher in the Capitol.

MENENIUS. Our very priests must become mockers if they shall encounter such ridiculous subjects as you are. When you speak best unto the purpose, it is not worth the wagging of your beards; and your beards deserve not so

honourable a grave as to stuff a botcher's cushion or to be
entombed in an ass's pack-saddle. Yet you must be saying,
Marcius is proud; who, in a cheap estimation, is worth all
your predecessors since Deucalion; though peradventure
some of the best of 'em were hereditary hangmen. God-den
to your worships: more of your conversation would infect
my brain, being the herdsmen of the beastly plebeians: I
will be bold to take my leave of you.

[BRUTUS and SICINIUS retire.]

[Enter VOLUMNIA, VIRGILIA, VALERIA, &c.]

How now, my as fair as noble ladies,—and the moon, were
she earthly, no nobler,—whither do you follow your eyes
so fast?

VOLUMNIA.
Honourable Menenius, my boy Marcius approaches; for the
love of
Juno, let's go.

MENENIUS.
Ha! Marcius coming home!

VOLUMNIA.
Ay, worthy Menenius, and with most prosperous approbation.

MENENIUS. Take my cap, Jupiter, and I thank thee.—Hoo!
Marcius coming home!

VOLUMNIA, VIRGILIA.
Nay, 'tis true.

VOLUMNIA. Look, here's a letter from him: the state hath
another, his wife another; and I think there's one at home
for you.

MENENIUS.
I will make my very house reel to-night.—A letter for me?

VIRGILIA.
Yes, certain, there's a letter for you; I saw it.

MENENIUS. A letter for me! It gives me an estate of seven years' health; in which time I will make a lip at the physician: the most sovereign prescription in Galen is but empiricutic, and, to this preservative, of no better report than a horse-drench. Is he not wounded? he was wont to come home wounded.

VIRGILIA.
O, no, no, no.

VOLUMNIA.
O, he is wounded, I thank the gods for't.

MENENIUS. So do I too, if it be not too much.—Brings a victory in his pocket?—The wounds become him.

VOLUMNIA. On's brows: Menenius, he comes the third time home with the oaken garland.

MENENIUS.
Has he disciplined Aufidius soundly?

VOLUMNIA. Titus Lartius writes,—they fought together, but Aufidius got off.

MENENIUS. And 'twas time for him too, I'll warrant him that: an he had stayed by him, I would not have been so fidiused for all the chests in Corioli and the gold that's in them. Is the Senate possessed of this?

VOLUMNIA. Good ladies, let's go.—Yes, yes, yes; the Senate has letters from the general, wherein he gives my son the whole name of the war: he hath in this action outdone his former deeds doubly.

VALERIA.
In troth, there's wondrous things spoke of him.

MENENIUS.
Wondrous! ay, I warrant you, and not without his true purchasing.

VIRGILIA.
The gods grant them true!

VOLUMNIA.
True! pow, wow.

MENENIUS. True! I'll be sworn they are true. Where is he
wounded?—[To the TRIBUNES, who come forward.] God
save your good worships! Marcius is coming home; he has
more cause to be proud.—Where is he wounded?

VOLUMNIA.
I' the shoulder and i' the left arm; there will be large
cicatrices to show the people when he shall stand for his
place.
He received in the repulse of Tarquin seven hurts i' the
body.

MENENIUS. One i' the neck and two i' the thigh,—there's
nine that I know.

VOLUMNIA.
He had, before this last expedition, twenty-five wounds
upon him.

MENENIUS.
Now it's twenty-seven: every gash was an enemy's grave.
[A shout and flourish.]
Hark! the trumpets.

VOLUMNIA.
These are the ushers of Marcius: before him
He carries noise, and behind him he leaves tears;
Death, that dark spirit, in's nervy arm doth lie;
Which, being advanc'd, declines, and then men die.

[A sennet. Trumpets sound. Enter COMINIUS and TITUS
LARTIUS; between them, CORIOLANUS, crowned with
an oaken garland; with CAPTAINS and Soldiers and a
HERALD.]

HERALD.
Know, Rome, that all alone Marcius did fight
Within Corioli gates: where he hath won,
With fame, a name to Caius Marcius; these
In honour follows Coriolanus:—
Welcome to Rome, renowned Coriolanus!

[Flourish.]

ALL.
  Welcome to Rome, renowned Coriolanus!

CORIOLANUS.
  No more of this, it does offend my heart;
  Pray now, no more.

COMINIUS.
  Look, sir, your mother!

CORIOLANUS.
  O,
  You have, I know, petition'd all the gods
  For my prosperity!

[Kneels.]

VOLUMNIA.
  Nay, my good soldier, up;
  My gentle Marcius, worthy Caius, and
  By deed-achieving honour newly nam'd,—
  What is it?—Coriolanus must I call thee?
  But, O, thy wife!

CORIOLANUS.
  My gracious silence, hail!
  Wouldst thou have laugh'd had I come coffin'd home,
  That weep'st to see me triumph? Ah, my dear,
  Such eyes the widows in Corioli wear,
  And mothers that lack sons.

MENENIUS.
  Now the gods crown thee!

CORIOLANUS.
  And live you yet? [To VALERIA]—O my sweet lady,
  pardon.

VOLUMNIA. I know not where to turn.—O, welcome
  home;—and welcome, general;—and you are welcome all.

MENENIUS.
    A hundred thousand welcomes.—I could weep
    And I could laugh; I am light and heavy.—Welcome:
    A curse begin at very root on's heart
    That is not glad to see thee!—You are three
    That Rome should dote on: yet, by the faith of men,
    We have some old crab trees here at home that will not
    Be grafted to your relish. Yet welcome, warriors.
    We call a nettle but a nettle; and
    The faults of fools but folly.

COMINIUS.
    Ever right.

CORIOLANUS.
    Menenius ever, ever.

HERALD.
    Give way there, and go on!

CORIOLANUS.
    [To his wife and mother.] Your hand, and yours:
    Ere in our own house I do shade my head,
    The good patricians must be visited;
    From whom I have receiv'd not only greetings,
    But with them change of honours.

VOLUMNIA.
    I have lived
    To see inherited my very wishes,
    And the buildings of my fancy; only
    There's one thing wanting, which I doubt not but
    Our Rome will cast upon thee.

CORIOLANUS.
    Know, good mother,
    I had rather be their servant in my way
    Than sway with them in theirs.

COMINIUS.
    On, to the Capitol.

[Flourish. Cornets. Exeunt in state, as before. The tribunes
    remain.]

BRUTUS.
  All tongues speak of him and the bleared sights
  Are spectacled to see him: your prattling nurse
  Into a rapture lets her baby cry
  While she chats him: the kitchen malkin pins
  Her richest lockram 'bout her reechy neck,
  Clamb'ring the walls to eye him: stalls, bulks, windows,
  Are smother'd up, leads fill'd and ridges hors'd
  With variable complexions; all agreeing
  In earnestness to see him: seld-shown flamens
  Do press among the popular throngs, and puff
  To win a vulgar station: our veil'd dames
  Commit the war of white and damask, in
  Their nicely gawded cheeks, to the wanton spoil
  Of Phoebus' burning kisses; such a pother,
  As if that whatsoever god who leads him
  Were slily crept into his human powers,
  And gave him graceful posture.

SICINIUS.
  On the sudden
  I warrant him consul.

BRUTUS.
  Then our office may
  During his power go sleep.

SICINIUS.
  He cannot temp'rately transport his honours
  From where he should begin and end; but will
  Lose those he hath won.

BRUTUS.
  In that there's comfort.

SICINIUS.
  Doubt not the commoners, for whom we stand,
  But they, upon their ancient malice will forget,
  With the least cause these his new honours; which
  That he will give them make as little question
  As he is proud to do't.

BRUTUS.
I heard him swear,
Were he to stand for consul, never would he
Appear i' the market-place, nor on him put
The napless vesture of humility;
Nor, showing, as the manner is, his wounds
To the people, beg their stinking breaths.

SICINIUS.
'Tis right.

BRUTUS.
It was his word: O, he would miss it rather
Than carry it but by the suit of the gentry to him,
And the desire of the nobles.

SICINIUS.
I wish no better
Than have him hold that purpose, and to put it
In execution.

BRUTUS.
'Tis most like he will.

SICINIUS.
It shall be to him then, as our good wills,
A sure destruction.

BRUTUS.
So it must fall out
To him or our authorities. For an end,
We must suggest the people in what hatred
He still hath held them; that to's power he would
Have made them mules, silenc'd their pleaders, and
Dispropertied their freedoms; holding them,
In human action and capacity,
Of no more soul nor fitness for the world
Than camels in their war; who have their provand
Only for bearing burdens, and sore blows
For sinking under them.

SICINIUS.
This, as you say, suggested
At some time when his soaring insolence

Shall touch the people,—which time shall not want,
If it be put upon't; and that's as easy
As to set dogs on sheep,—will be his fire
To kindle their dry stubble; and their blaze
Shall darken him for ever.

[Enter A MESSENGER.]

BRUTUS.
What's the matter?

MESSENGER.
You are sent for to the Capitol. 'Tis thought
That Marcius shall be consul:
I have seen the dumb men throng to see him, and
The blind to hear him speak: matrons flung gloves,
Ladies and maids their scarfs and handkerchers,
Upon him as he pass'd; the nobles bended
As to Jove's statue; and the commons made
A shower and thunder with their caps and shouts:
I never saw the like.

BRUTUS.
Let's to the Capitol;
And carry with us ears and eyes for the time,
But hearts for the event.

SICINIUS.
Have with you.

[Exeunt.]

SCENE II. ROME. THE CAPITOL.

[Enter two OFFICERS, to lay cushions.]

FIRST OFFICER.
Come, come; they are almost here. How many stand for
consulships?

SECOND OFFICER. Three, they say; but 'tis thought of
every one Coriolanus will carry it.

FIRST OFFICER. That's a brave fellow; but he's vengeance
proud and loves not the common people.

SECOND OFFICER. Faith, there have been many great men
that have flattered the people, who ne'er loved them; and
there be many that they have loved, they know not wherefore; so that, if they love they know not why, they hate
upon no better a ground: therefore, for Coriolanus neither
to care whether they love or hate him manifests the true
knowledge he has in their disposition; and, out of his noble
carelessness, lets them plainly see't.

FIRST OFFICER. If he did not care whether he had their
love or no, he waved indifferently 'twixt doing them
neither good nor harm; but he seeks their hate with greater
devotion than they can render it him; and leaves nothing
undone that may fully discover him their opposite. Now to
seem to affect the malice and displeasure of the people is
as bad as that which he dislikes,—to flatter them for their
love.

SECOND OFFICER. He hath deserved worthily of his
country: and his ascent is not by such easy degrees as those
who, having been supple and courteous to the people,
bonnetted, without any further deed to have them at all,
into their estimation and report: but he hath so planted his
honours in their eyes, and his actions in their hearts, that
for their tongues to be silent, and not confess so much,
were a kind of ingrateful injury; to report otherwise were a
malice that, giving itself the lie, would pluck reproof and
rebuke from every ear that heard it.

FIRST OFFICER.
No more of him; he is a worthy man.: make way, they are
coming.

[A sennet. Enter, with Lictors before them, COMINIUS the
Consul,
MENENIUS, CORIOLANUS, Senators, SICINIUS and
BRUTUS. The Senators

take their places; the Tribunes take theirs also by themselves.]

MENENIUS.
Having determined of the Volsces, and
To send for Titus Lartius, it remains,

As the main point of this our after-meeting,
To gratify his noble service that
Hath thus stood for his country: therefore please you,
Most reverend and grave elders, to desire
The present consul, and last general
In our well-found successes, to report
A little of that worthy work perform'd
By Caius Marcius Coriolanus; whom
We met here both to thank and to remember
With honours like himself.

FIRST SENATOR.
Speak, good Cominius:
Leave nothing out for length, and make us think
Rather our state's defective for requital
Than we to stretch it out.—Masters o' the people,
We do request your kindest ears; and, after,
Your loving motion toward the common body,
To yield what passes here.

SICINIUS.
We are convented
Upon a pleasing treaty; and have hearts
Inclinable to honour and advance
The theme of our assembly.

BRUTUS.
Which the rather
We shall be bless'd to do, if he remember
A kinder value of the people than
He hath hereto priz'd them at.

MENENIUS.
That's off, that's off;
I would you rather had been silent. Please you
To hear Cominius speak?

BRUTUS.
Most willingly.
But yet my caution was more pertinent
Than the rebuke you give it.

MENENIUS.
  He loves your people;
  But tie him not to be their bedfellow.—
  Worthy Cominius, speak.

[CORIOLANUS rises, and offers to go away.]

Nay, keep your place.

FIRST SENATOR.
  Sit, Coriolanus; never shame to hear
  What you have nobly done.

CORIOLANUS.
  Your Honours' pardon:
  I had rather have my wounds to heal again
  Than hear say how I got them.

BRUTUS.
  Sir, I hope
  My words disbench'd you not.

CORIOLANUS.
  No, sir; yet oft,
  When blows have made me stay, I fled from words.
  You sooth'd not, therefore hurt not: but your people,
  I love them as they weigh.

MENENIUS.
  Pray now, sit down.

CORIOLANUS.
  I had rather have one scratch my head i' the sun
  When the alarum were struck, than idly sit
  To hear my nothings monster'd.

[Exit.]

MENENIUS.
  Masters o' the people,
  Your multiplying spawn how can he flatter,—
  That's thousand to one good one,—when you now see
  He had rather venture all his limbs for honour
  Than one on's ears to hear it?—Proceed, Cominius.

COMINIUS.
I shall lack voice: the deeds of Coriolanus
Should not be utter'd feebly.—It is held
That valour is the chiefest virtue, and
Most dignifies the haver: if it be,
The man I speak of cannot in the world
Be singly counterpois'd. At sixteen years,
When Tarquin made a head for Rome, he fought
Beyond the mark of others; our then dictator,
Whom with all praise I point at, saw him fight,
When with his Amazonian chin he drove
The bristled lips before him: he bestrid
An o'erpress'd Roman and i' the consul's view
Slew three opposers: Tarquin's self he met,
And struck him on his knee: in that day's feats,
When he might act the woman in the scene,
He proved best man i' the field, and for his meed
Was brow-bound with the oak. His pupil age
Man-enter'd thus, he waxed like a sea;
And in the brunt of seventeen battles since
He lurch'd all swords of the garland. For this last,
Before and in Corioli, let me say,
I cannot speak him home: he stopp'd the fliers;
And by his rare example made the coward
Turn terror into sport: as weeds before
A vessel under sail, so men obey'd,
And fell below his stem: his sword,—death's stamp,—
Where it did mark, it took; from face to foot
He was a thing of blood, whose every motion
Was timed with dying cries: alone he enter'd
The mortal gate of the city, which he painted
With shunless destiny; aidless came off,
And with a sudden re-enforcement struck
Corioli like a planet. Now all's his:
When, by and by, the din of war 'gan pierce
His ready sense; then straight his doubled spirit
Re-quick'ned what in flesh was fatigate,
And to the battle came he; where he did
Run reeking o'er the lives of men, as if
'Twere a perpetual spoil: and till we call'd
Both field and city ours he never stood
To ease his breast with panting.

MENENIUS.
  Worthy man!

FIRST SENATOR.
  He cannot but with measure fit the honours
  Which we devise him.

COMINIUS.
  Our spoils he kick'd at;
  And looked upon things precious as they were
  The common muck of the world: he covets less
  Than misery itself would give; rewards
  His deeds with doing them; and is content
  To spend the time to end it.

MENENIUS.
  He's right noble:
  Let him be call'd for.

FIRST SENATOR.
  Call Coriolanus.

OFFICER.
  He doth appear.

[Re-enter CORIOLANUS.]

MENENIUS.
  The Senate, Coriolanus, are well pleas'd
  To make thee consul.

CORIOLANUS.
  I do owe them still
  My life and services.

MENENIUS.
  It then remains
  That you do speak to the people.

CORIOLANUS.
  I do beseech you
  Let me o'erleap that custom; for I cannot
  Put on the gown, stand naked, and entreat them,
  For my wounds' sake to give their suffrage: please you
  That I may pass this doing.

SICINIUS.
  Sir, the people
  Must have their voices; neither will they bate
  One jot of ceremony.

MENENIUS.
  Put them not to't:—
  Pray you, go fit you to the custom; and
  Take to you, as your predecessors have,
  Your honour with your form.

CORIOLANUS.
  It is a part
  That I shall blush in acting, and might well
  Be taken from the people.

BRUTUS.
  Mark you that?

CORIOLANUS.
  To brag unto them,—thus I did, and thus;—
  Show them the unaching scars which I should hide,
  As if I had receiv'd them for the hire
  Of their breath only!

MENENIUS.
  Do not stand upon't.—
  We recommend to you, tribunes of the people,
  Our purpose to them;—and to our noble consul
  Wish we all joy and honour.

SENATORS.
  To Coriolanus come all joy and honour!

[Flourish. Exeunt all but SICINIUS and BRUTUS.]

BRUTUS.
  You see how he intends to use the people.

SICINIUS.
  May they perceive's intent! He will require them
  As if he did contemn what he requested
  Should be in them to give.

BRUTUS.
Come, we'll inform them
Of our proceedings here: on the market-place
I know they do attend us.

[Exeunt.]

SCENE III. ROME. THE FORUM.

[Enter several citizens.]

FIRST CITIZEN.
Once, if he do require our voices, we ought not to deny
him.

SECOND CITIZEN.
We may, sir, if we will.

THIRD CITIZEN. We have power in ourselves to do it, but
it is a power that we have no power to do: for if he show us
his wounds and tell us his deeds, we are to put our tongues
into those wounds and speak for them; so, if he tell us his
noble deeds, we must also tell him our noble acceptance
of them. Ingratitude is monstrous: and for the multitude to
be ingrateful were to make a monster of the multitude; of
the which we being members, should bring ourselves to be
monstrous members.

FIRST CITIZEN. And to make us no better thought of, a
little help will serve; for once we stood up about the corn,
he himself stuck not to call us the many-headed multitude.

THIRD CITIZEN. We have been called so of many; not that
our heads are some brown, some black, some auburn, some
bald, but that our wits are so diversely coloured; and truly
I think if all our wits were to issue out of one skull, they
would fly east, west, north, south; and their consent of one
direct way should be at once to all the points o' the com-
pass.

SECOND CITIZEN.
Think you so? Which way do you judge my wit would fly?

THIRD CITIZEN. Nay, your wit will not so soon out as another man's will,—'tis strongly wedged up in a block-head; but if it were at liberty 'twould, sure, southward.

SECOND CITIZEN.
  Why that way?

THIRD CITIZEN. To lose itself in a fog; where being three parts melted away with rotten dews, the fourth would return for conscience' sake, to help to get thee a wife.

SECOND CITIZEN.
  You are never without your tricks:—you may, you may.

THIRD CITIZEN. Are you all resolved to give your voices? But that's no matter, the greater part carries it. I say, if he would incline to the people, there was never a worthier man. Here he comes, and in the gown of humility. Mark his behaviour. We are not to stay all together, but to come by him where he stands, by ones, by twos, and by threes. He's to make his requests by particulars, wherein every one of us has a single honour, in giving him our own voices with our own tongues; therefore follow me, and I'll direct you how you shall go by him.

ALL.
  Content, content.

[Exeunt.]

[Enter CORIOLANUS and MENENIUS.]

MENENIUS.
  O sir, you are not right; have you not known
  The worthiest men have done't!

CORIOLANUS.
  What must I say?—
  'I pray, sir'—Plague upon't! I cannot bring
  My tongue to such a pace.—'Look, sir,—my wounds;—
  I got them in my country's service, when
  Some certain of your brethren roar'd, and ran
  From the noise of our own drums.'

MENENIUS.
  O me, the gods!
  You must not speak of that: you must desire them
  To think upon you.

CORIOLANUS.
  Think upon me! Hang 'em!
  I would they would forget me, like the virtues
  Which our divines lose by 'em.

MENENIUS.
  You'll mar all:
  I'll leave you. Pray you speak to 'em, I pray you,
  In wholesome manner.

CORIOLANUS.
  Bid them wash their faces
  And keep their teeth clean.

[Exit MENENIUS.]

So, here comes a brace:

[Re-enter two citizens.]

You know the cause, sirs, of my standing here.

FIRST CITIZEN.
  We do, sir; tell us what hath brought you to't.

CORIOLANUS.
  Mine own desert.

SECOND CITIZEN.
  Your own desert?

CORIOLANUS.
  Ay, not mine own desire.

FIRST CITIZEN.
  How! not your own desire!

CORIOLANUS. No, sir, 'twas never my desire yet to trouble
  the poor with begging.

FIRST CITIZEN.
You must think, if we give you anything, we hope to gain by you.

CORIOLANUS.
Well then, I pray, your price o' the consulship?

FIRST CITIZEN.
The price is to ask it kindly.

CORIOLANUS. Kindly! sir, I pray, let me ha't: I have wounds to show you, which shall be yours in private.— Your good voice, sir; what say you?

SECOND CITIZEN.
You shall ha' it, worthy sir.

CORIOLANUS. A match, sir.—There's in all two worthy voices begg'd.—I have your alms: adieu.

FIRST CITIZEN.
But this is something odd.

SECOND CITIZEN.
An 'twere to give again,— but 'tis no matter.

[Exeunt two citizens.]

[Re-enter other two citizens.]

CORIOLANUS. Pray you now, if it may stand with the tune of your voices that I may be consul, I have here the customary gown.

THIRD CITIZEN. You have deserved nobly of your country, and you have not deserved nobly.

CORIOLANUS.
Your enigma?

THIRD CITIZEN. You have been a scourge to her enemies; you have been a rod to her friends: you have not indeed loved the common people.

CORIOLANUS. You should account me the more virtuous, that I have not been common in my love. I will, sir, flatter my sworn brother, the people, to earn a dearer estimation of them; 'tis a condition they account gentle: and since the wisdom of their choice is rather to have my hat than my heart, I will practise the insinuating nod and be off to them most counterfeitly: that is, sir, I will counterfeit the be-witchment of some popular man and give it bountifully to the desirers. Therefore, beseech you, I may be consul.

FOURTH CITIZEN. We hope to find you our friend; and therefore give you our voices heartily.

THIRD CITIZEN.
You have received many wounds for your country.

CORIOLANUS. I will not seal your knowledge with show-ing them. I will make much of your voices, and so trouble you no further.

BOTH CITIZENS.
The gods give you joy, sir, heartily!

[Exeunt citizens.]

CORIOLANUS.
Most sweet voices!—
Better it is to die, better to starve,
Than crave the hire which first we do deserve.
Why in this wolvish toge should I stand here,
To beg of Hob and Dick that do appear,
Their needless vouches? custom calls me to't:—
What custom wills, in all things should we do't,
The dust on antique time would lie unswept,
And mountainous error be too highly heap'd
For truth to o'erpeer. Rather than fool it so,
Let the high office and the honour go
To one that would do thus.—I am half through;
The one part suffer'd, the other will I do.
Here come more voices.

[Re-enter other three citizens.]

Your voices: for your voices I have fought;

Watch'd for your voices; for your voices bear
Of wounds two dozen odd; battles thrice six
I have seen and heard of; for your voices have
Done many things, some less, some more: your voices:
Indeed, I would be consul.

FIFTH CITIZEN.
He has done nobly, and cannot go without any honest
man's voice.

SIXTH CITIZEN. Therefore let him be consul: the gods give
him joy, and make him good friend to the people!

ALL THREE CITIZENS.
Amen, amen.—God save thee, noble consul!

[Exeunt.]

CORIOLANUS.
Worthy voices!

[Re-enter MENENIUS, with BRUTUS and SICINIUS.]

MENENIUS.
You have stood your limitation; and the tribunes
Endue you with the people's voice:—remains
That, in the official marks invested, you
Anon do meet the senate.

CORIOLANUS.
Is this done?

SICINIUS.
The custom of request you have discharg'd:
The people do admit you; and are summon'd
To meet anon, upon your approbation.

CORIOLANUS.
Where? at the senate-house?

SICINIUS.
There, Coriolanus.

CORIOLANUS.
May I change these garments?

SICINIUS.
  You may, sir.

CORIOLANUS.
  That I'll straight do; and, knowing myself again,
  Repair to the senate-house.

MENENIUS.
  I'll keep you company.—Will you along?

BRUTUS.
  We stay here for the people.

SICINIUS.
  Fare you well.

[Exeunt CORIOLANUS and MENENIUS.]

He has it now; and by his looks methinks
  'Tis warm at his heart.

BRUTUS.
  With a proud heart he wore his humble weeds.
  Will you dismiss the people?

[Re-enter citizens.]

SICINIUS.
  How now, my masters! have you chose this man?

FIRST CITIZEN.
  He has our voices, sir.

BRUTUS.
  We pray the gods he may deserve your loves.

SECOND CITIZEN.
  Amen, sir:—to my poor unworthy notice,
  He mocked us when he begg'd our voices.

THIRD CITIZEN.
  Certainly;
  He flouted us downright.

FIRST CITIZEN.
  No, 'tis his kind of speech,—he did not mock us.

SECOND CITIZEN.
Not one amongst us, save yourself, but says
He us'd us scornfully: he should have show'd us
His marks of merit, wounds received for's country.

SICINIUS.
Why, so he did, I am sure.

CITIZENS.
No, no; no man saw 'em.

THIRD CITIZEN.
He said he had wounds, which he could show in private;
And with his hat, thus waving it in scorn,
'I would be consul,' says he; 'aged custom
But by your voices, will not so permit me;
Your voices therefore:' when we granted that,
Here was, 'I thank you for your voices,—thank you,—
Your most sweet voices:—now you have left your voices
I have no further with you:'—was not this mockery?

SICINIUS.
Why either were you ignorant to see't?
Or, seeing it, of such childish friendliness
To yield your voices?

BRUTUS.
Could you not have told him,
As you were lesson'd,—when he had no power,
But was a petty servant to the state,
He was your enemy; ever spake against
Your liberties, and the charters that you bear
I' the body of the weal: and now, arriving
A place of potency and sway o' the state,
If he should still malignantly remain
Fast foe to the plebeii, your voices might
Be curses to yourselves? You should have said,
That as his worthy deeds did claim no less
Than what he stood for, so his gracious nature
Would think upon you for your voices, and
Translate his malice towards you into love,
Standing your friendly lord.

SICINIUS.
  Thus to have said,
  As you were fore-advis'd, had touch'd his spirit
  And tried his inclination; from him pluck'd
  Either his gracious promise, which you might,
  As cause had call'd you up, have held him to;
  Or else it would have gall'd his surly nature,
  Which easily endures not article
  Tying him to aught; so, putting him to rage,
  You should have ta'en the advantage of his choler
  And pass'd him unelected.

BRUTUS.
  Did you perceive
  He did solicit you in free contempt
  When he did need your loves; and do you think
  That his contempt shall not be bruising to you
  When he hath power to crush? Why, had your bodies
  No heart among you? Or had you tongues to cry
  Against the rectorship of judgment?

SICINIUS.
  Have you
  Ere now denied the asker, and now again,
  Of him that did not ask but mock, bestow
  Your su'd-for tongues?

THIRD CITIZEN.
  He's not confirm'd: we may deny him yet.

SECOND CITIZEN.
  And will deny him:
  I'll have five hundred voices of that sound.

FIRST CITIZEN.
  I twice five hundred, and their friends to piece 'em.

BRUTUS.
  Get you hence instantly; and tell those friends
  They have chose a consul that will from them take
  Their liberties, make them of no more voice
  Than dogs, that are as often beat for barking
  As therefore kept to do so.

SICINIUS.

Let them assemble;
And, on a safer judgment, all revoke
Your ignorant election: enforce his pride
And his old hate unto you: besides, forget not
With what contempt he wore the humble weed;
How in his suit he scorn'd you: but your loves,
Thinking upon his services, took from you
Th' apprehension of his present portance,
Which, most gibingly, ungravely, he did fashion
After the inveterate hate he bears you.

BRUTUS.

Lay
A fault on us, your tribunes; that we labour'd,—
No impediment between,—but that you must
Cast your election on him.

SICINIUS.

Say you chose him
More after our commandment than as guided
By your own true affections; and that your minds,
Pre-occupied with what you rather must do
Than what you should, made you against the grain
To voice him consul. Lay the fault on us.

BRUTUS.

Ay, spare us not. Say we read lectures to you,
How youngly he began to serve his country,
How long continued: and what stock he springs of—
The noble house o' the Marcians; from whence came
That Ancus Marcius, Numa's daughter's son,
Who, after great Hostilius, here was king;
Of the same house Publius and Quintus were,
That our best water brought by conduits hither;
And Censorinus, darling of the people,
And nobly nam'd so, twice being censor,
Was his great ancestor.

SICINIUS.

One thus descended,
That hath beside well in his person wrought
To be set high in place, we did commend

To your remembrances: but you have found,
Scaling his present bearing with his past,
That he's your fixed enemy, and revoke
Your sudden approbation.

BRUTUS.
Say you ne'er had done't,—
Harp on that still,—but by our putting on:
And presently when you have drawn your number,
Repair to the Capitol.

CITIZENS.
We will so; almost all
Repent in their election.

[Exeunt.]

BRUTUS.
Let them go on;
This mutiny were better put in hazard
Than stay, past doubt, for greater:
If, as his nature is, he fall in rage
With their refusal, both observe and answer
The vantage of his anger.

SICINIUS.
To the Capitol,
Come: we will be there before the stream o' the people;
And this shall seem, as partly 'tis, their own,
Which we have goaded onward.

[Exeunt.]

ACT III.

[Cornets. Enter CORIOLANUS, MENENIUS, COMINIUS,
  TITUS LARTIUS,
  Senators, and Patricians.]

CORIOLANUS.
  Tullus Aufidius, then, had made new head?

LARTIUS.
  He had, my lord; and that it was which caus'd
  Our swifter composition.

CORIOLANUS.
  So then the Volsces stand but as at first;
  Ready, when time shall prompt them, to make road
  Upon's again.

COMINIUS.
  They are worn, lord consul, so
  That we shall hardly in our ages see
  Their banners wave again.

CORIOLANUS.
  Saw you Aufidius?

LARTIUS.
  On safeguard he came to me; and did curse
  Against the Volsces, for they had so vilely
  Yielded the town; he is retir'd to Antium.

CORIOLANUS.
  Spoke he of me?

LARTIUS.
  He did, my lord.

CORIOLANUS.
  How? What?

LARTIUS.
  How often he had met you, sword to sword;
  That of all things upon the earth he hated
  Your person most; that he would pawn his fortunes
  To hopeless restitution, so he might
  Be call'd your vanquisher.

CORIOLANUS.
  At Antium lives he?

LARTIUS.
  At Antium.

CORIOLANUS.
  I wish I had a cause to seek him there,
  To oppose his hatred fully.—Welcome home. [To Laertes.]

[Enter SICINIUS and BRUTUS.]

Behold! these are the tribunes of the people;
  The tongues o' the common mouth. I do despise them,
  For they do prank them in authority,
  Against all noble sufferance.

SICINIUS.
  Pass no further.

CORIOLANUS.
  Ha! what is that?

BRUTUS.
  It will be dangerous to go on: no further.

CORIOLANUS.
  What makes this change?

MENENIUS.
  The matter?

COMINIUS.
  Hath he not pass'd the noble and the commons?

BRUTUS.
  Cominius, no.

CORIOLANUS.
Have I had children's voices?

FIRST SENATOR.
Tribunes, give way; he shall to the market-place.

BRUTUS.
The people are incens'd against him.

SICINIUS.
Stop,
Or all will fall in broil.

CORIOLANUS.
Are these your herd?—
Must these have voices, that can yield them now,
And straight disclaim their tongues?—What are your offic-
es?
You being their mouths, why rule you not their teeth?
Have you not set them on?

MENENIUS.
Be calm, be calm.

CORIOLANUS.
It is a purpos'd thing, and grows by plot,
To curb the will of the nobility:
Suffer't, and live with such as cannot rule,
Nor ever will be rul'd.

BRUTUS.
Call't not a plot:
The people cry you mock'd them; and of late,
When corn was given them gratis, you repin'd;
Scandal'd the suppliants for the people,—call'd them
Time-pleasers, flatterers, foes to nobleness.

CORIOLANUS.
Why, this was known before.

BRUTUS.
Not to them all.

CORIOLANUS.
Have you inform'd them sithence?

BRUTUS.
  How! I inform them!

COMINIUS.
  You are like to do such business.

BRUTUS.
  Not unlike,
  Each way, to better yours.

CORIOLANUS.
  Why, then, should I be consul? By yond clouds,
  Let me deserve so ill as you, and make me
  Your fellow tribune.

SICINIUS.
  You show too much of that
  For which the people stir: if you will pass
  To where you are bound, you must inquire your way,
  Which you are out of, with a gentler spirit;
  Or never be so noble as a consul,
  Nor yoke with him for tribune.

MENENIUS.
  Let's be calm.

COMINIUS.
  The people are abus'd; set on. This palt'ring
  Becomes not Rome; nor has Coriolanus
  Deserv'd this so dishonour'd rub, laid falsely
  I' the plain way of his merit.

CORIOLANUS.
  Tell me of corn!
  This was my speech, and I will speak't again,—

MENENIUS.
  Not now, not now.

FIRST SENATOR.
  Not in this heat, sir, now.

CORIOLANUS.
  Now, as I live, I will.—My nobler friends,
  I crave their pardons:

For the mutable, rank-scented many, let them
Regard me as I do not flatter, and
Therein behold themselves: I say again,
In soothing them we nourish 'gainst our senate
The cockle of rebellion, insolence, sedition,
Which we ourselves have plough'd for, sow'd, and scatter'd,
By mingling them with us, the honour'd number,
Who lack not virtue, no, nor power, but that
Which they have given to beggars.

MENENIUS.
　Well, no more.

FIRST SENATOR.
　No more words, we beseech you.

CORIOLANUS.
　How! no more!
　As for my country I have shed my blood,
　Not fearing outward force, so shall my lungs
　Coin words till their decay against those measles
　Which we disdain should tetter us, yet sought
　The very way to catch them.

BRUTUS.
　You speak o' the people
　As if you were a god, to punish, not
　A man of their infirmity.

SICINIUS.
　'Twere well
　We let the people know't.

MENENIUS.
　What, what? his choler?

CORIOLANUS.
　Choler!
　Were I as patient as the midnight sleep,
　By Jove, 'twould be my mind!

SICINIUS.
  It is a mind
  That shall remain a poison where it is,
  Not poison any further.

CORIOLANUS.
  Shall remain!—
  Hear you this Triton of the minnows? mark you
  His absolute 'shall'?

COMINIUS.
  'Twas from the canon.

CORIOLANUS.
  'Shall'!
  O good, but most unwise patricians! why,
  You grave but reckless senators, have you thus
  Given Hydra leave to choose an officer,
  That with his peremptory 'shall,' being but
  The horn and noise o' the monster, wants not spirit
  To say he'll turn your current in a ditch,
  And make your channel his? If he have power,
  Then vail your ignorance: if none, awake
  Your dangerous lenity. If you are learn'd,
  Be not as common fools; if you are not,
  Let them have cushions by you. You are plebeians,
  If they be senators: and they are no less
  When, both your voices blended, the great'st taste
  Most palates theirs. They choose their magistrate;
  And such a one as he, who puts his 'shall,'
  His popular 'shall,' against a graver bench
  Than ever frown'd in Greece. By Jove himself,
  It makes the consuls base: and my soul aches
  To know, when two authorities are up,
  Neither supreme, how soon confusion
  May enter 'twixt the gap of both and take
  The one by the other.

COMINIUS.
  Well, on to the market-place.

CORIOLANUS.
  Whoever gave that counsel, to give forth
  The corn o' the storehouse gratis, as 'twas us'd
  Sometime in Greece,—

MENENIUS.
  Well, well, no more of that.

CORIOLANUS.
  Though there the people had more absolute power,—
  I say they nourish'd disobedience, fed
  The ruin of the state.

BRUTUS.
  Why shall the people give
  One that speaks thus their voice?

CORIOLANUS.
  I'll give my reasons,
  More worthier than their voices. They know the corn
  Was not our recompense, resting well assur'd
  They ne'er did service for't; being press'd to the war,
  Even when the navel of the state was touch'd,
  They would not thread the gates,—this kind of service
  Did not deserve corn gratis: being i' the war,
  Their mutinies and revolts, wherein they show'd
  Most valour, spoke not for them. The accusation
  Which they have often made against the senate,
  All cause unborn, could never be the motive
  Of our so frank donation. Well, what then?
  How shall this bisson multitude digest
  The senate's courtesy? Let deeds express
  What's like to be their words:—'We did request it;
  We are the greater poll, and in true fear
  They gave us our demands:'— Thus we debase
  The nature of our seats, and make the rabble
  Call our cares fears; which will in time
  Break ope the locks o' the senate and bring in
  The crows to peck the eagles.—

MENENIUS.
  Come, enough.

BRUTUS.
  Enough, with over-measure.

CORIOLANUS.
  No, take more:
  What may be sworn by, both divine and human,
  Seal what I end withal!—This double worship,—
  Where one part does disdain with cause, the other
  Insult without all reason; where gentry, title, wisdom,
  Cannot conclude but by the yea and no
  Of general ignorance—it must omit
  Real necessities, and give way the while
  To unstable slightness: purpose so barr'd, it follows,
  Nothing is done to purpose. Therefore, beseech you,—
  You that will be less fearful than discreet;
  That love the fundamental part of state
  More than you doubt the change on't; that prefer
  A noble life before a long, and wish
  To jump a body with a dangerous physic
  That's sure of death without it,—at once pluck out
  The multitudinous tongue; let them not lick
  The sweet which is their poison: your dishonour
  Mangles true judgment, and bereaves the state
  Of that integrity which should become't;
  Not having the power to do the good it would,
  For the ill which doth control't.

BRUTUS.
  Has said enough.

SICINIUS.
  Has spoken like a traitor, and shall answer
  As traitors do.

CORIOLANUS.
  Thou wretch, despite o'erwhelm thee!—
  What should the people do with these bald tribunes?
  On whom depending, their obedience fails
  To the greater bench: in a rebellion,
  When what's not meet, but what must be, was law,
  Then were they chosen; in a better hour
  Let what is meet be said it must be meet,
  And throw their power i' the dust.

BRUTUS.
  Manifest treason!

SICINIUS.
  This a consul? no.

BRUTUS.
  The aediles, ho!—Let him be apprehended.

SICINIUS.
  Go call the people [Exit BRUTUS.]; in whose name myself
  Attach thee as a traitorous innovator,
  A foe to the public weal. Obey, I charge thee,
  And follow to thine answer.

CORIOLANUS.
  Hence, old goat!

SENATORS and PATRICIANS.
  We'll surety him.

COMINIUS.
  Aged sir, hands off.

CORIOLANUS.
  Hence, rotten thing! or I shall shake thy bones
  Out of thy garments.

SICINIUS.
  Help, ye citizens!

[Re-enter Brutus, with the AEDILES and a rabble of Citizens.]

MENENIUS.
  On both sides more respect.

SICINIUS.
  Here's he that would take from you all your power.

BRUTUS.
  Seize him, aediles.

PLEBEIANS.
  Down with him! down with him!

SECOND SENATOR.
  Weapons, weapons, weapons!

[They all bustle about CORIOLANUS.]

Tribunes! patricians! citizens!—What, ho!—
  Sicinius, Brutus, Coriolanus, Citizens!

CITIZENS.
  Peace, peace, peace; stay, hold, peace!

MENENIUS.
  What is about to be?—I am out of breath;
  Confusion's near: I cannot speak.—You tribunes
  To the people,—Coriolanus, patience:—
  Speak, good Sicinius.

SICINIUS.
  Hear me, people: peace!

CITIZENS.
  Let's hear our tribune: peace!—
  Speak, speak, speak.

SICINIUS.
  You are at point to lose your liberties;
  Marcius would have all from you; Marcius,
  Whom late you have nam'd for consul.

MENENIUS.
  Fie, fie, fie!
  This is the way to kindle, not to quench.

FIRST SENATOR.
  To unbuild the city, and to lay all flat.

SICINIUS.
  What is the city but the people?
CITIZENS.
  True,
  The people are the city.

BRUTUS.
  By the consent of all, we were establish'd
  The people's magistrates.

CITIZENS.
You so remain.

MENENIUS.
And so are like to do.

COMINIUS.
That is the way to lay the city flat;
To bring the roof to the foundation,
And bury all which yet distinctly ranges,
In heaps and piles of ruin.

SICINIUS.
This deserves death.

BRUTUS.
Or let us stand to our authority,
Or let us lose it.—We do here pronounce,
Upon the part o' the people, in whose power
We were elected theirs, Marcius is worthy
Of present death.

SICINIUS.
Therefore lay hold of him;
Bear him to the rock Tarpeian, and from thence
Into destruction cast him.

BRUTUS.
Aediles, seize him!

CITIZENS.
Yield, Marcius, yield!

MENENIUS.
Hear me one word;
Beseech you, tribunes, hear me but a word.

AEDILES.
Peace, peace!

MENENIUS.
Be that you seem, truly your country's friends,
And temperately proceed to what you would
Thus violently redress.

BRUTUS.
  Sir, those cold ways,
  That seem like prudent helps, are very poisonous
  Where the disease is violent.—Lay hands upon him
  And bear him to the rock.

CORIOLANUS.
  No; I'll die here. [Draws his sword.]
  There's some among you have beheld me fighting;
  Come, try upon yourselves what you have seen me.

MENENIUS.
  Down with that sword!—Tribunes, withdraw awhile.

BRUTUS.
  Lay hands upon him.

MENENIUS.
  Help Marcius, help,
  You that be noble; help him, young and old!

CITIZENS.
  Down with him, down with him!

[In this mutiny the TRIBUNES, the AEDILES, and the people are beat in.]

MENENIUS.
  Go, get you to your house; be gone, away!
  All will be nought else.

SECOND SENATOR.
  Get you gone.

CORIOLANUS.
  Stand fast;
  We have as many friends as enemies.

MENENIUS.
  Shall it be put to that?

FIRST SENATOR.
  The gods forbid:
  I pr'ythee, noble friend, home to thy house;
  Leave us to cure this cause.

MENENIUS.
For 'tis a sore upon us
You cannot tent yourself; be gone, beseech you.

COMINIUS.
Come, sir, along with us.

CORIOLANUS.
I would they were barbarians,—as they are,
Though in Rome litter'd,—not Romans,—as they are not,
Though calv'd i' the porch o' the Capitol.

MENENIUS.
Be gone;
Put not your worthy rage into your tongue;
One time will owe another.

CORIOLANUS.
On fair ground
I could beat forty of them.

MENENIUS.
I could myself
Take up a brace o' the best of them; yea, the two tribunes.

COMINIUS.
But now 'tis odds beyond arithmetic;
And manhood is call'd foolery when it stands
Against a falling fabric.—Will you hence,
Before the tag return? whose rage doth rend
Like interrupted waters, and o'erbear
What they are used to bear.

MENENIUS.
Pray you be gone:
I'll try whether my old wit be in request
With those that have but little: this must be patch'd
With cloth of any colour.

COMINIUS.
Nay, come away.

[Exeunt CORIOLANUS, COMINIUS, and others.]

FIRST PATRICIAN.
  This man has marr'd his fortune.

MENENIUS.
  His nature is too noble for the world:
  He would not flatter Neptune for his trident,
  Or Jove for's power to thunder. His heart's his mouth:
  What his breast forges, that his tongue must vent;
  And, being angry, does forget that ever
  He heard the name of death.

[A noise within.]

Here's goodly work!

SECOND PATRICIAN.
  I would they were a-bed!

MENENIUS.
  I would they were in Tiber!
  What the vengeance, could he not speak 'em fair?

[Re-enter BRUTUS and SICINIUS, with the rabble.]

SICINIUS.
  Where is this viper
  That would depopulate the city and
  Be every man himself?

MENENIUS.
  You worthy tribunes,—

SICINIUS.
  He shall be thrown down the Tarpeian rock
  With rigorous hands: he hath resisted law,
  And therefore law shall scorn him further trial
  Than the severity of the public power,
  Which he so sets at nought.

FIRST CITIZEN.
  He shall well know
  The noble tribunes are the people's mouths,
  And we their hands.

CITIZENS.
  He shall, sure on't.

MENENIUS.
  Sir, sir,—

SICINIUS.
  Peace!

MENENIUS.
  Do not cry havoc, where you should but hunt
  With modest warrant.

SICINIUS.
  Sir, how comes't that you
  Have holp to make this rescue?

MENENIUS.
  Hear me speak:—
  As I do know the consul's worthiness,
  So can I name his faults,—

SICINIUS.
  Consul!—what consul?

MENENIUS.
  The consul Coriolanus.

BRUTUS.
  He consul!

CITIZENS.
  No, no, no, no, no.

MENENIUS.
  If, by the tribunes' leave, and yours, good people,
  I may be heard, I would crave a word or two;
  The which shall turn you to no further harm
  Than so much loss of time.

SICINIUS.
  Speak briefly, then;
  For we are peremptory to dispatch
  This viperous traitor: to eject him hence
  Were but one danger; and to keep him here

Our certain death: therefore it is decreed
He dies to-night.

MENENIUS.
Now the good gods forbid
That our renowned Rome, whose gratitude
Towards her deserved children is enroll'd
In Jove's own book, like an unnatural dam
Should now eat up her own!

SICINIUS.
He's a disease that must be cut away.

MENENIUS.
O, he's a limb that has but a disease;
Mortal, to cut it off; to cure it, easy.
What has he done to Rome that's worthy death?
Killing our enemies, the blood he hath lost,—
Which I dare vouch is more than that he hath
By many an ounce,—he dropt it for his country;
And what is left, to lose it by his country
Were to us all, that do't and suffer it
A brand to the end o' the world.

SICINIUS.
This is clean kam.

BRUTUS.
Merely awry: when he did love his country,
It honour'd him.

MENENIUS.
The service of the foot,
Being once gangren'd, is not then respected
For what before it was.

BRUTUS.
We'll hear no more.—
Pursue him to his house, and pluck him thence;
Lest his infection, being of catching nature,
Spread further.

MENENIUS.
  One word more, one word.
  This tiger-footed rage, when it shall find
  The harm of unscann'd swiftness, will, too late,
  Tie leaden pounds to's heels. Proceed by process;
  Lest parties,—as he is belov'd,—break out,
  And sack great Rome with Romans.

BRUTUS.
  If it were so,—

SICINIUS.
  What do ye talk?
  Have we not had a taste of his obedience?
  Our aediles smote? ourselves resisted?—come,—

MENENIUS.
  Consider this:—he has been bred i' the wars
  Since 'a could draw a sword, and is ill school'd
  In bolted language; meal and bran together
  He throws without distinction. Give me leave,
  I'll go to him and undertake to bring him
  Where he shall answer, by a lawful form,
  In peace, to his utmost peril.

FIRST SENATOR.
  Noble tribunes,
  It is the humane way: the other course
  Will prove too bloody; and the end of it
  Unknown to the beginning.

SICINIUS.
  Noble Menenius,
  Be you then as the people's officer.—
  Masters, lay down your weapons.

BRUTUS.
  Go not home.

SICINIUS.
  Meet on the market-place.—We'll attend you there:
  Where, if you bring not Marcius, we'll proceed
  In our first way.

MENENIUS.
  I'll bring him to you.—
  [To the SENATORS.] Let me desire your company: he
  must come,
  Or what is worst will follow.

FIRST SENATOR.
  Pray you let's to him.

[Exeunt.]

SCENE II. ROME. A ROOM IN CORIOLANUS'S HOUSE.

[Enter CORIOLANUS and Patricians.]

CORIOLANUS.
  Let them pull all about mine ears; present me
  Death on the wheel, or at wild horses' heels;
  Or pile ten hills on the Tarpeian rock,
  That the precipitation might down stretch
  Below the beam of sight; yet will I still
  Be thus to them.

FIRST PATRICIAN.
  You do the nobler.

CORIOLANUS.
  I muse my mother
  Does not approve me further, who was wont
  To call them woollen vassals, things created
  To buy and sell with groats; to show bare heads
  In congregations, to yawn, be still, and wonder,
  When one but of my ordinance stood up
  To speak of peace or war.

[Enter VOLUMNIA.]

I talk of you: [To Volumnia.]
  Why did you wish me milder? Would you have me
  False to my nature? Rather say, I play
  The man I am.

VOLUMNIA.
O, sir, sir, sir,
I would have had you put your power well on
Before you had worn it out.

CORIOLANUS.
Let go.

VOLUMNIA.
You might have been enough the man you are
With striving less to be so: lesser had been
The thwartings of your dispositions, if
You had not show'd them how ye were dispos'd,
Ere they lack'd power to cross you.

CORIOLANUS.
Let them hang.

VOLUMNIA.
Ay, and burn too.

[Enter MENENIUS with the SENATORS.]

MENENIUS.
Come, come, you have been too rough, something too
rough;
You must return and mend it.

FIRST SENATOR.
There's no remedy;
Unless, by not so doing, our good city
Cleave in the midst, and perish.

VOLUMNIA.
Pray be counsell'd;
I have a heart as little apt as yours,
But yet a brain that leads my use of anger
To better vantage.

MENENIUS.
Well said, noble woman!
Before he should thus stoop to the herd, but that
The violent fit o' the time craves it as physic
For the whole state, I would put mine armour on,
Which I can scarcely bear.

CORIOLANUS.
  What must I do?

MENENIUS.
  Return to the tribunes.

CORIOLANUS.
  Well, what then? what then?

MENENIUS.
  Repent what you have spoke.

CORIOLANUS.
  For them?—I cannot do it to the gods;
  Must I then do't to them?

VOLUMNIA.
  You are too absolute;
  Though therein you can never be too noble
  But when extremities speak. I have heard you say
  Honour and policy, like unsever'd friends,
  I' the war do grow together: grant that, and tell me
  In peace what each of them by th' other lose
  That they combine not there.

CORIOLANUS.
  Tush, tush!

MENENIUS.
  A good demand.

VOLUMNIA.
  If it be honour in your wars to seem
  The same you are not,—which for your best ends
  You adopt your policy,—how is it less or worse
  That it shall hold companionship in peace
  With honour as in war; since that to both
  It stands in like request?

CORIOLANUS.
  Why force you this?

VOLUMNIA.
  Because that now it lies you on to speak
  To the people; not by your own instruction,

Nor by the matter which your heart prompts you,
But with such words that are but rooted in
Your tongue, though but bastards and syllables
Of no allowance, to your bosom's truth.
Now, this no more dishonours you at all
Than to take in a town with gentle words,
Which else would put you to your fortune and
The hazard of much blood.
I would dissemble with my nature where
My fortunes and my friends at stake requir'd
I should do so in honour: I am in this
Your wife, your son, these senators, the nobles;
And you will rather show our general louts
How you can frown, than spend a fawn upon 'em
For the inheritance of their loves and safeguard
Of what that want might ruin.

MENENIUS.
Noble lady!—
Come, go with us; speak fair: you may salve so,
Not what is dangerous present, but the loss
Of what is past.

VOLUMNIA.
I pr'ythee now, my son,
Go to them with this bonnet in thy hand;
And thus far having stretch'd it,—here be with them,—
Thy knee bussing the stones,—for in such busines
Action is eloquence, and the eyes of the ignorant
More learned than the ears,—waving thy head,
Which often, thus correcting thy stout heart,
Now humble as the ripest mulberry
That will not hold the handling: or say to them
Thou art their soldier, and, being bred in broils,
Hast not the soft way which, thou dost confess,
Were fit for thee to use, as they to claim,
In asking their good loves; but thou wilt frame
Thyself, forsooth, hereafter theirs, so far
As thou hast power and person.

MENENIUS.
This but done
Even as she speaks, why, their hearts were yours:
For they have pardons, being ask'd, as free
As words to little purpose.

VOLUMNIA.
Pr'ythee now,
Go, and be rul'd; although I know thou had'st rather
Follow thine enemy in a fiery gulf
Than flatter him in a bower.

[Enter COMINIUS.]

Here is Cominius.

COMINIUS.
I have been i' the market-place; and, sir, 'tis fit
You make strong party, or defend yourself
By calmness or by absence: all's in anger.

MENENIUS.
Only fair speech.

COMINIUS.
I think 'twill serve, if he
Can thereto frame his spirit.

VOLUMNIA.
He must, and will.—
Pr'ythee now, say you will, and go about it.

CORIOLANUS.
Must I go show them my unbarb'd sconce? must I
With my base tongue, give to my noble heart
A lie, that it must bear? Well, I will do't:
Yet, were there but this single plot to lose,
This mould of Marcius, they to dust should grind it,
And throw't against the wind.—To the market-place:—
You have put me now to such a part which never
I shall discharge to the life.

COMINIUS.
Come, come, we'll prompt you.

VOLUMNIA.
  I pr'ythee now, sweet son,—as thou hast said
  My praises made thee first a soldier, so,
  To have my praise for this, perform a part
  Thou hast not done before.

CORIOLANUS.
  Well, I must do't:
  Away, my disposition, and possess me
  Some harlot's spirit! My throat of war be turn'd,
  Which quired with my drum, into a pipe
  Small as an eunuch, or the virgin voice
  That babies lulls asleep! the smiles of knaves
  Tent in my cheeks; and school-boys' tears take up
  The glasses of my sight! a beggar's tongue
  Make motion through my lips; and my arm'd knees,
  Who bow'd but in my stirrup, bend like his
  That hath receiv'd an alms!—I will not do't;
  Lest I surcease to honour mine own truth,
  And by my body's action teach my mind
  A most inherent baseness.

VOLUMNIA.
  At thy choice, then:
  To beg of thee, it is my more dishonour
  Than thou of them. Come all to ruin: let
  Thy mother rather feel thy pride than fear
  Thy dangerous stoutness; for I mock at death
  With as big heart as thou. Do as thou list.
  Thy valiantness was mine, thou suck'dst it from me;
  But owe thy pride thyself.

CORIOLANUS.
  Pray, be content:
  Mother, I am going to the market-place;
  Chide me no more. I'll mountebank their loves,
  Cog their hearts from them, and come home belov'd
  Of all the trades in Rome. Look, I am going.
  Commend me to my wife. I'll return consul;
  Or never trust to what my tongue can do
  I' the way of flattery further.

VOLUMNIA.
  Do your will.

[Exit.]

COMINIUS.
  Away! The tribunes do attend you: arm yourself
  To answer mildly; for they are prepar'd
  With accusations, as I hear, more strong
  Than are upon you yet.

CORIOLANUS.
  The word is, mildly.—Pray you let us go:
  Let them accuse me by invention, I
  Will answer in mine honour.

MENENIUS.
  Ay, but mildly.

CORIOLANUS.
  Well, mildly be it then; mildly.

[Exeunt.]

SCENE III. ROME. THE FORUM.

[Enter SICINIUS and BRUTUS.]

BRUTUS.
  In this point charge him home, that he affects
  Tyrannical power: if he evade us there,
  Enforce him with his envy to the people;
  And that the spoil got on the Antiates
  Was ne'er distributed.

[Enter an AEDILE.]

What, will he come?

AEDILE.
  He's coming.

BRUTUS.
  How accompanied?

AEDILE.
  With old Menenius, and those senators
  That always favour'd him.

SICINIUS.
  Have you a catalogue
  Of all the voices that we have procur'd,
  Set down by the poll?

AEDILE.
  I have; 'tis ready.

SICINIUS.
  Have you collected them by tribes?

AEDILE.
  I have.

SICINIUS.
  Assemble presently the people hither:
  And when they hear me say 'It shall be so
  I' the right and strength o' the commons,' be it either
  For death, for fine, or banishment, then let them,
  If I say fine, cry 'Fine!'- if death, cry 'Death;'
  Insisting on the old prerogative
  And power i' the truth o' the cause.

AEDILE.
  I shall inform them.

BRUTUS.
  And when such time they have begun to cry,
  Let them not cease, but with a din confus'd
  Enforce the present execution
  Of what we chance to sentence.

AEDILE.
  Very well.

SICINIUS.
  Make them be strong, and ready for this hint,
  When we shall hap to give't them.

BRUTUS.
  Go about it.

[Exit AEDILE.]
Put him to choler straight: he hath been us'd
Ever to conquer, and to have his worth
Of contradiction; being once chaf'd, he cannot
Be rein'd again to temperance; then he speaks
What's in his heart; and that is there which looks
With us to break his neck.

SICINIUS.
Well, here he comes.

[Enter CORIOLANUS, MENENIUS, COMINIUS, Senators,
and Patricians.]

MENENIUS.
Calmly, I do beseech you.

CORIOLANUS.
Ay, as an ostler, that for the poorest piece
Will bear the knave by the volume.—The honoured gods
Keep Rome in safety, and the chairs of justice
Supplied with worthy men! plant love among's!
Throng our large temples with the shows of peace,
And not our streets with war!

FIRST SENATOR.
Amen, amen!

MENENIUS.
A noble wish.

[Re-enter the AEDILE, with Citizens.]

SICINIUS.
Draw near, ye people.

AEDILE.
List to your tribunes; audience: peace, I say!

CORIOLANUS.
First, hear me speak.

BOTH TRIBUNES.
Well, say.—Peace, ho!

CORIOLANUS.
Shall I be charg'd no further than this present?
Must all determine here?

SICINIUS.
I do demand,
If you submit you to the people's voices,
Allow their officers, and are content
To suffer lawful censure for such faults
As shall be proved upon you.

CORIOLANUS.
I am content.

MENENIUS.
Lo, citizens, he says he is content:
The warlike service he has done, consider; think
Upon the wounds his body bears, which show
Like graves i' the holy churchyard.

CORIOLANUS.
Scratches with briers,
Scars to move laughter only.

MENENIUS.
Consider further,
That when he speaks not like a citizen,
You find him like a soldier: do not take
His rougher accents for malicious sounds,
But, as I say, such as become a soldier,
Rather than envy you.

COMINIUS.
Well, well, no more.

CORIOLANUS.
What is the matter,
That being pass'd for consul with full voice,
I am so dishonour'd that the very hour
You take it off again?

SICINIUS.
Answer to us.

CORIOLANUS.
  Say then: 'tis true, I ought so.

SICINIUS.
  We charge you that you have contriv'd to take
  From Rome all season'd office, and to wind
  Yourself into a power tyrannical;
  For which you are a traitor to the people.

CORIOLANUS.
  How! traitor!

MENENIUS.
  Nay, temperately; your promise.

CORIOLANUS.
  The fires i' the lowest hell fold in the people!
  Call me their traitor!—Thou injurious tribune!
  Within thine eyes sat twenty thousand deaths,
  In thy hands clutch'd as many millions, in
  Thy lying tongue both numbers, I would say,
  Thou liest unto thee with a voice as free
  As I do pray the gods.

SICINIUS.
  Mark you this, people?

CITIZENS.
  To the rock, to the rock, with him!

SICINIUS.
  Peace!
  We need not put new matter to his charge:
  What you have seen him do and heard him speak,
  Beating your officers, cursing yourselves,
  Opposing laws with strokes, and here defying
  Those whose great power must try him; even this,
  So criminal and in such capital kind,
  Deserves the extremest death.

BRUTUS.
  But since he hath
  Serv'd well for Rome,—

CORIOLANUS.
What do you prate of service?

BRUTUS.
I talk of that that know it.

CORIOLANUS.
You?

MENENIUS.
Is this the promise that you made your mother?

COMINIUS.
Know, I pray you,—

CORIOLANUS.
I'll know no further:
Let them pronounce the steep Tarpeian death,
Vagabond exile, flaying, pent to linger
But with a grain a day, I would not buy
Their mercy at the price of one fair word,
Nor check my courage for what they can give,
To have't with saying Good-morrow.

SICINIUS.
For that he has,—
As much as in him lies,—from time to time
Envied against the people, seeking means
To pluck away their power; as now at last
Given hostile strokes, and that not in the presence
Of dreaded justice, but on the ministers
That do distribute it;—in the name o' the people,
And in the power of us the tribunes, we,
Even from this instant, banish him our city,
In peril of precipitation
From off the rock Tarpeian, never more
To enter our Rome gates: I' the people's name,
I say it shall be so.

CITIZENS.
It shall be so, it shall be so; let him away;
He's banished, and it shall be so.

COMINIUS.
  Hear me, my masters and my common friends,—

SICINIUS.
  He's sentenc'd; no more hearing.

COMINIUS.
  Let me speak:
  I have been consul, and can show for Rome
  Her enemies' marks upon me. I do love
  My country's good with a respect more tender,
  More holy and profound, than mine own life,
  My dear wife's estimate, her womb's increase,
  And treasure of my loins; then if I would
  Speak that,—

SICINIUS.
  We know your drift. Speak what?

BRUTUS.
  There's no more to be said, but he is banish'd,
  As enemy to the people and his country:
  It shall be so.

CITIZENS.
  It shall be so, it shall be so.

CORIOLANUS.
  You common cry of curs! whose breath I hate
  As reek o' the rotten fens, whose loves I prize
  As the dead carcasses of unburied men
  That do corrupt my air,—I banish you;
  And here remain with your uncertainty!
  Let every feeble rumour shake your hearts!
  Your enemies, with nodding of their plumes,
  Fan you into despair! Have the power still
  To banish your defenders; till at length
  Your ignorance,—which finds not till it feels,—
  Making but reservation of yourselves,—
  Still your own foes,—deliver you, as most
  Abated captives to some nation
  That won you without blows! Despising,
  For you, the city, thus I turn my back:
  There is a world elsewhere.

[Exeunt CORIOLANUS, COMINIUS, MENENIUS, Senators, and
  Patricians.]

AEDILE.
  The people's enemy is gone, is gone!

CITIZENS.
  Our enemy is banish'd, he is gone! Hoo! hoo!

[Shouting, and throwing up their caps.]

SICINIUS.
  Go, see him out at gates, and follow him,
  As he hath follow'd you, with all despite;
  Give him deserv'd vexation. Let a guard
  Attend us through the city.

CITIZENS.
  Come, come, let's see him out at gates; come.
  The gods preserve our noble tribunes! Come.

[Exeunt.]

ACT IV.

SCENE I. ROME. BEFORE A GATE OF THE CITY.

[Enter CORIOLANUS, VOLUMNIA, VIRGILIA, MENE-
NIUS, COMINIUS,and several young Patricians.]

CORIOLANUS.
  Come, leave your tears; a brief farewell:—he beast
  With many heads butts me away.—Nay, mother,
  Where is your ancient courage? you were us'd
  To say extremities was the trier of spirits;
  That common chances common men could bear;
  That when the sea was calm all boats alike
  Show'd mastership in floating; fortune's blows,
  When most struck home, being gentle wounded, craves
  A noble cunning; you were us'd to load me
  With precepts that would make invincible
  The heart that conn'd them.

VIRGILIA.
  O heavens! O heavens!

CORIOLANUS.
  Nay, I pr'ythee, woman,—

VOLUMNIA.
  Now the red pestilence strike all trades in Rome,
  And occupations perish!

CORIOLANUS.
  What, what, what!
  I shall be lov'd when I am lack'd. Nay, mother,
  Resume that spirit when you were wont to say,
  If you had been the wife of Hercules,
  Six of his labours you'd have done, and sav'd
  Your husband so much sweat.—Cominius,
  Droop not; adieu.—Farewell, my wife,—my mother:
  I'll do well yet.—Thou old and true Menenius,
  Thy tears are salter than a younger man's,

And venomous to thine eyes.—My sometime general,
I have seen thee stern, and thou hast oft beheld
Heart-hard'ning spectacles; tell these sad women
'Tis fond to wail inevitable strokes,
As 'tis to laugh at 'em.—My mother, you wot well
My hazards still have been your solace: and
Believe't not lightly,—though I go alone,
Like to a lonely dragon, that his fen
Makes fear'd and talk'd of more than seen,—your son
Will or exceed the common or be caught
With cautelous baits and practice.

VOLUMNIA.
  My first son,
  Whither wilt thou go? Take good Cominius
  With thee awhile: determine on some course
  More than a wild exposture to each chance
  That starts i' the way before thee.

CORIOLANUS.
  O the gods!

COMINIUS.
  I'll follow thee a month, devise with thee
  Where thou shalt rest, that thou mayst hear of us,
  And we of thee: so, if the time thrust forth
  A cause for thy repeal, we shall not send
  O'er the vast world to seek a single man;
  And lose advantage, which doth ever cool
  I' the absence of the needer.

CORIOLANUS.
  Fare ye well:
  Thou hast years upon thee; and thou art too full
  Of the wars' surfeits to go rove with one
  That's yet unbruis'd: bring me but out at gate.—
  Come, my sweet wife, my dearest mother, and
  My friends of noble touch; when I am forth,
  Bid me farewell, and smile. I pray you, come.
  While I remain above the ground, you shall
  Hear from me still; and never of me aught
  But what is like me formerly.

MENENIUS.
That's worthily
As any ear can hear.—Come, let's not weep.—
If I could shake off but one seven years
From these old arms and legs, by the good gods,
I'd with thee every foot.

CORIOLANUS.
Give me thy hand:—
Come.

[Exeunt.]

SCENE II. ROME. A STREET NEAR THE GATE.

[Enter SICINIUS, BRUTUS, and an AEDILE.]

SICINIUS.
Bid them all home; he's gone, and we'll no further.—
The nobility are vex'd, whom we see have sided
In his behalf.

BRUTUS.
Now we have shown our power,
Let us seem humbler after it is done
Than when it was a-doing.

SICINIUS.
Bid them home:
Say their great enemy is gone, and they
Stand in their ancient strength.

BRUTUS.
Dismiss them home.

[Exit AEDILE.]

Here comes his mother.

SICINIUS.
Let's not meet her.

BRUTUS.
Why?

SICINIUS.
They say she's mad.

BRUTUS.
They have ta'en note of us: keep on your way.

[Enter VOLUMNIA, VIRGILIA, and MENENIUS.]

VOLUMNIA.
O, you're well met: the hoarded plague o' the gods
Requite your love!

MENENIUS.
Peace, peace, be not so loud.

VOLUMNIA.
If that I could for weeping, you should hear,—
Nay, and you shall hear some.—[To BRUTUS.] Will you
be gone?

VIRGILIA.
You shall stay too[To SICINIUS.]: I would I had the power
To say so to my husband.

SICINIUS.
Are you mankind?

VOLUMNIA.
Ay, fool; is that a shame?—Note but this, fool.—
Was not a man my father? Hadst thou foxship
To banish him that struck more blows for Rome
Than thou hast spoken words?—

SICINIUS.
O blessed heavens!

VOLUMNIA.
Moe noble blows than ever thou wise words;
And for Rome's good.—I'll tell thee what;—yet go;—
Nay, but thou shalt stay too:—I would my son
Were in Arabia, and thy tribe before him,
His good sword in his hand.

SICINIUS.
What then?

VIRGILIA.
What then!
He'd make an end of thy posterity.

VOLUMNIA.
Bastards and all.—
Good man, the wounds that he does bear for Rome!

MENENIUS.
Come, come, peace.

SICINIUS.
I would he had continu'd to his country
As he began, and not unknit himself
The noble knot he made.

BRUTUS.
I would he had.

VOLUMNIA.
I would he had! 'Twas you incens'd the rabble;—
Cats, that can judge as fitly of his worth
As I can of those mysteries which heaven
Will not have earth to know.

BRUTUS.
Pray, let us go.

VOLUMNIA.
Now, pray, sir, get you gone:
You have done a brave deed. Ere you go, hear this,—
As far as doth the Capitol exceed
The meanest house in Rome, so far my son,—
This lady's husband here; this, do you see?—
Whom you have banish'd does exceed you all.

BRUTUS.
Well, well, we'll leave you.

SICINIUS.
Why stay we to be baited
With one that wants her wits?

VOLUMNIA.
Take my prayers with you.—

[Exeunt TRIBUNES.]

I would the gods had nothing else to do
  But to confirm my curses! Could I meet 'em
  But once a day, it would unclog my heart
  Of what lies heavy to't.

MENENIUS.
  You have told them home,
  And, by my troth, you have cause. You'll sup with me?

VOLUMNIA.
  Anger's my meat; I sup upon myself,
  And so shall starve with feeding.—Come, let's go:
  Leave this faint puling and lament as I do,
  In anger, Juno-like. Come, come, come.

[Exeunt.]

MENENIUS.
  Fie, fie, fie!

SCENE III. A HIGHWAY BETWEEN ROME AND ANTIUM.

[Enter a ROMAN and a VOLSCE, meeting.]

ROMAN. I know you well, sir, and you know me; your
  name, I think, is Adrian.

VOLSCE.
  It is so, sir: truly, I have forgot you.

ROMAN. I am a Roman; and my services are, as you are,
  against 'em: know you me yet?

VOLSCE.
  Nicanor? no!

ROMAN.
  The same, sir.

VOLSCE. You had more beard when I last saw you; but your
  favour is well approved by your tongue. What's the news
  in Rome? I have a note from the Volscian state, to find you
  out there; you have well saved me a day's journey.

ROMAN. There hath been in Rome strange insurrections: the people against the senators, patricians, and nobles.

VOLSCE. Hath been! is it ended, then? Our state thinks not so; they are in a most warlike preparation, and hope to come upon them in the heat of their division.

ROMAN. The main blaze of it is past, but a small thing would make it flame again; for the nobles receive so to heart the banishment of that worthy Coriolanus that they are in a ripe aptness to take all power from the people, and to pluck from them their tribunes for ever. This lies glowing, I can tell you, and is almost mature for the violent breaking out.

VOLSCE.
Coriolanus banished!

ROMAN.
Banished, sir.

VOLSCE.
You will be welcome with this intelligence, Nicanor.

ROMAN. The day serves well for them now. I have heard it said the fittest time to corrupt a man's wife is when she's fallen out with her husband. Your noble Tullus Aufidius will appear well in these wars, his great opposer, Coriolanus, being now in no request of his country.

VOLSCE. He cannot choose. I am most fortunate thus accidentally to encounter you; you have ended my business, and I will merrily accompany you home.

ROMAN. I shall between this and supper tell you most strange things from Rome; all tending to the good of their adversaries. Have you an army ready, say you?

VOLSCE. A most royal one; the centurions and their charges, distinctly billeted, already in the entertainment, and to be on foot at an hour's warning.

ROMAN. I am joyful to hear of their readiness, and am the man, I think, that shall set them in present action. So, sir, heartily well met, and most glad of your company.

VOLSCE. You take my part from me, sir; I have the most
cause to be glad of yours.

ROMAN.
Well, let us go together.

[Exeunt.]

SCENE IV. ANTIUM. BEFORE AUFIDIUS'S HOUSE.

[Enter CORIOLANUS, in mean apparel, disguised and
muffled.]

CORIOLANUS.
A goodly city is this Antium. City,
'Tis I that made thy widows: many an heir
Of these fair edifices 'fore my wars
Have I heard groan and drop: then know me not.
Lest that thy wives with spits and boys with stones,
In puny battle slay me.

[Enter a CITIZEN.]

Save you, sir.

CITIZEN.
And you.

CORIOLANUS.
Direct me, if it be your will,
Where great Aufidius lies; is he in Antium?

CITIZEN.
He is, and feasts the nobles of the state
At his house this night.

CORIOLANUS.
Which is his house, beseech you?

CITIZEN.
This, here, before you.

CORIOLANUS.
Thank you, sir; farewell.

[Exit CITIZEN.]

O world, thy slippery turns! Friends now fast sworn,
  Whose double bosoms seems to wear one heart,
  Whose hours, whose bed, whose meal and exercise
  Are still together, who twin, as 'twere, in love
  Unseparable, shall within this hour,
  On a dissension of a doit, break out
  To bitterest enmity; so fellest foes,
  Whose passions and whose plots have broke their sleep
  To take the one the other, by some chance,
  Some trick not worth an egg, shall grow dear friends
  And interjoin their issues. So with me:—
  My birthplace hate I, and my love's upon
  This enemy town.—I'll enter; if he slay me,
  He does fair justice; if he give me way,
  I'll do his country service.

SCENE V. ANTIUM. A HALL IN AUFIDIUS'S HOUSE.

[Music within. Enter A SERVANT.]

FIRST SERVANT.
  Wine, wine, wine! What service is here!
  I think our fellows are asleep.

[Exit.]

[Enter a second SERVANT.]

SECOND SERVANT.
  Where's Cotus? my master calls for him.—Cotus!

[Exit.]

[Enter CORIOLANUS.]

CORIOLANUS.
  A goodly house: the feast smells well; but I
  Appear not like a guest.

[Re-enter the first SERVANT.]

FIRST SERVANT. What would you have, friend? whence
  are you? Here's no place for you: pray go to the door.

CORIOLANUS.
I have deserv'd no better entertainment
In being Coriolanus.

[Re-enter second SERVANT.]

SECOND SERVANT. Whence are you, sir? Has the porter
his eyes in his head that he gives entrance to such compan-
ions? Pray, get you out.

CORIOLANUS.
Away!

SECOND SERVANT.
Away? Get you away.

CORIOLANUS.
Now the art troublesome.

SECOND SERVANT.
Are you so brave? I'll have you talked with anon.

[Enter a third SERVANT. The first meets him.]

THIRD SERVANT.
What fellow's this?

FIRST SERVANT. A strange one as ever I looked on: I
cannot get him out o' the house. Pr'ythee call my master to
him.

THIRD SERVANT.
What have you to do here, fellow? Pray you avoid the
house.

CORIOLANUS.
Let me but stand; I will not hurt your hearth.

THIRD SERVANT.
What are you?

CORIOLANUS.
A gentleman.

THIRD SERVANT.
A marvellous poor one.

CORIOLANUS.
  True, so I am.

THIRD SERVANT. Pray you, poor gentleman, take up some
  other station; here's no place for you. Pray you avoid;
  come.

CORIOLANUS.
  Follow your function, go,
  And batten on cold bits.

[Pushes him away.]

THIRD SERVANT. What, you will not?—Pr'ythee, tell my
  master what a strange guest he has here.

SECOND SERVANT.
  And I shall.

[Exit.]

THIRD SERVANT.
  Where dwell'st thou?

CORIOLANUS.
  Under the canopy.

THIRD SERVANT.
  Under the canopy?

CORIOLANUS.
  Ay.

THIRD SERVANT.
  Where's that?

CORIOLANUS.
  I' the city of kites and crows.

THIRD SERVANT. I' the city of kites and crows!—What an
  ass it is!—Then thou dwell'st with daws too?

CORIOLANUS.
  No, I serve not thy master.

THIRD SERVANT.
  How, sir! Do you meddle with my master?

CORIOLANUS.
  Ay; 'tis an honester service than to meddle with thy mis-
  tress.
  Thou prat'st and prat'st; serve with thy trencher, hence!

[Beats him away.]

[Enter AUFIDIUS and the second SERVANT.]

AUFIDIUS.
  Where is this fellow?

SECOND SERVANT. Here, sir; I'd have beaten him like a
  dog, but for disturbing the lords within.

AUFIDIUS.
  Whence com'st thou? what wouldst thou? thy name?
  Why speak'st not? speak, man: what's thy name?

CORIOLANUS.
  [Unmuffling.] If, Tullus,
  Not yet thou know'st me, and, seeing me, dost not
  Think me for the man I am, necessity
  Commands me name myself.

AUFIDIUS.
  What is thy name?

[Servants retire.]

CORIOLANUS.
  A name unmusical to the Volscians' ears,
  And harsh in sound to thine.

AUFIDIUS.
  Say, what's thy name?
  Thou has a grim appearance, and thy face
  Bears a command in't; though thy tackle's torn,
  Thou show'st a noble vessel: what's thy name?

CORIOLANUS.
  Prepare thy brow to frown:—know'st thou me yet?

AUFIDIUS.
  I know thee not:—thy name?

CORIOLANUS.
  My name is Caius Marcius, who hath done
  To thee particularly, and to all the Volsces,
  Great hurt and mischief; thereto witness may
  My surname, Coriolanus: the painful service,
  The extreme dangers, and the drops of blood
  Shed for my thankless country, are requited
  But with that surname; a good memory,
  And witness of the malice and displeasure
  Which thou shouldst bear me: only that name remains;
  The cruelty and envy of the people,
  Permitted by our dastard nobles, who
  Have all forsook me, hath devour'd the rest,
  And suffer'd me by the voice of slaves to be
  Whoop'd out of Rome. Now, this extremity
  Hath brought me to thy hearth: not out of hope,
  Mistake me not, to save my life; for if
  I had fear'd death, of all the men i' the world
  I would have 'voided thee; but in mere spite,
  To be full quit of those my banishers,
  Stand I before thee here. Then if thou hast
  A heart of wreak in thee, that wilt revenge
  Thine own particular wrongs, and stop those maims
  Of shame seen through thy country, speed thee straight
  And make my misery serve thy turn: so use it
  That my revengeful services may prove
  As benefits to thee; for I will fight
  Against my canker'd country with the spleen
  Of all the under fiends. But if so be
  Thou dar'st not this, and that to prove more fortunes
  Th'art tir'd, then, in a word, I also am
  Longer to live most weary, and present
  My throat to thee and to thy ancient malice;
  Which not to cut would show thee but a fool,
  Since I have ever follow'd thee with hate,
  Drawn tuns of blood out of thy country's breast,
  And cannot live but to thy shame, unless
  It be to do thee service.

AUFIDIUS.
  O Marcius, Marcius!
  Each word thou hast spoke hath weeded from my heart
  A root of ancient envy. If Jupiter
  Should from yond cloud speak divine things,
  And say ''Tis true,' I'd not believe them more
  Than thee, all noble Marcius.—Let me twine
  Mine arms about that body, where against
  My grained ash an hundred times hath broke
  And scar'd the moon with splinters; here I clip
  The anvil of my sword, and do contest
  As hotly and as nobly with thy love
  As ever in ambitious strength I did
  Contend against thy valour. Know thou first,
  I lov'd the maid I married; never man
  Sighed truer breath; but that I see thee here,
  Thou noble thing! more dances my rapt heart
  Than when I first my wedded mistress saw
  Bestride my threshold. Why, thou Mars! I tell thee
  We have a power on foot; and I had purpose
  Once more to hew thy target from thy brawn,
  Or lose mine arm for't: thou hast beat me out
  Twelve several times, and I have nightly since
  Dreamt of encounters 'twixt thyself and me;
  We have been down together in my sleep,
  Unbuckling helms, fisting each other's throat,
  And wak'd half dead with nothing. Worthy Marcius,
  Had we no other quarrel else to Rome, but that
  Thou art thence banish'd, we would muster all
  From twelve to seventy; and, pouring war
  Into the bowels of ungrateful Rome,
  Like a bold flood o'erbear. O, come, go in,
  And take our friendly senators by the hands;
  Who now are here, taking their leaves of me,
  Who am prepar'd against your territories,
  Though not for Rome itself.

CORIOLANUS.
  You bless me, gods!

AUFIDIUS.
  Therefore, most absolute sir, if thou wilt have

The leading of thine own revenges, take
Th' one half of my commission; and set down,—
As best thou art experienc'd, since thou know'st
Thy country's strength and weakness,—thine own ways;
Whether to knock against the gates of Rome,
Or rudely visit them in parts remote,
To fright them, ere destroy. But come in;
Let me commend thee first to those that shall
Say yea to thy desires. A thousand welcomes!
And more a friend than e'er an enemy;
Yet, Marcius, that was much. Your hand: most welcome!

[Exeunt CORIOLANUS and AUFIDIUS.]

FIRST SERVANT.
  Here's a strange alteration!

SECOND SERVANT. By my hand, I had thought to have
  strucken him with a cudgel; and yet my mind gave me his
  clothes made a false report of him.

FIRST SERVANT. What an arm he has! He turned me about
  with his finger and his thumb, as one would set up a top.

SECOND SERVANT. Nay, I knew by his face that there
  was something in him; he had, sir, a kind of face,
  methought,—I cannot tell how to term it.

FIRST SERVANT. He had so, looking as it were,—would
  I were hanged, but I thought there was more in him than I
  could think.

SECOND SERVANT. So did I, I'll be sworn: he is simply
  the rarest man i' the world.

FIRST SERVANT.
  I think he is; but a greater soldier than he you wot on.

SECOND SERVANT.
  Who, my master?

FIRST SERVANT.
  Nay, it's no matter for that.

SECOND SERVANT.
  Worth six on him.

FIRST SERVANT.
  Nay, not so neither: but I take him to be the greater soldier.

SECOND SERVANT. Faith, look you, one cannot tell how to
  say that: for the defence of a town our general is excellent.

FIRST SERVANT.
  Ay, and for an assault too.

[Re-enter third SERVANT.]

THIRD SERVANT.
  O slaves, I can tell you news,—news, you rascals!

FIRST and SECOND SERVANT.
  What, what, what? let's partake.

THIRD SERVANT. I would not be a Roman, of all nations; I
  had as lief be a condemned man.

FIRST and SECOND SERVANT.
  Wherefore? wherefore?

THIRD SERVANT.
  Why, here's he that was wont to thwack our general,—Cai-
  us
  Marcius.

FIRST SERVANT.
  Why do you say, thwack our general?

THIRD SERVANT. I do not say thwack our general; but he
  was always good enough for him.

SECOND SERVANT. Come, we are fellows and friends: he
  was ever too hard for him; I have heard him say so himself.

FIRST SERVANT.
  He was too hard for him directly, to say the troth on't;
  before
  Corioli he scotched him and notched him like a carbonado.

SECOND SERVANT. An he had been cannibally given, he
   might have broiled and eaten him too.

FIRST SERVANT.
   But more of thy news?

THIRD SERVANT. Why, he is so made on here within as if
   he were son and heir to Mars; set at upper end o' the table:
   no question asked him by any of the senators but they stand
   bald before him: our general himself makes a mistress of
   him, sanctifies himself with's hand, and turns up the white
   o' the eye to his discourse. But the bottom of the news is,
   our general is cut i' the middle, and but one half of what he
   was yesterday; for the other has half, by the entreaty and
   grant of the whole table. He'll go, he says, and sowl the
   porter of Rome gates by the ears; he will mow all down
   before him, and leave his passage polled.

SECOND SERVANT.
   And he's as like to do't as any man I can imagine.

THIRD SERVANT. Do't! he will do't; for look you, sir, he
   has as many friends as enemies; which friends, sir, as it
   were, durst not, look you, sir, show themselves, as we term
   it, his friends, whilst he's in dejectitude.

FIRST SERVANT.
   Dejectitude! what's that?

THIRD SERVANT. But when they shall see, sir, his crest up
   again, and the man in blood, they will out of their burrows,
   like conies after rain, and revel all with him.

FIRST SERVANT.
   But when goes this forward?

THIRD SERVANT. To-morrow; to-day; presently; you shall
   have the drum struck up this afternoon: 'tis as it were
   parcel of their feast, and to be executed ere they wipe their
   lips.

SECOND SERVANT. Why, then we shall have a stirring
   world again. This peace is nothing but to rust iron, increase
   tailors, and breed ballad-makers.

FIRST SERVANT. Let me have war, say I; it exceeds peace
as far as day does night; it's spritely, waking, audible, and
full of vent. Peace is a very apoplexy, lethargy; mulled,
deaf, sleepy, insensible; a getter of more bastard children
than war's a destroyer of men.

SECOND SERVANT. 'Tis so: and as war in some sort, may
be said to be a ravisher, so it cannot be denied but peace is
a great maker of cuckolds.

FIRST SERVANT.
Ay, and it makes men hate one another.

THIRD SERVANT. Reason: because they then less need one
another. The wars for my money. I hope to see Romans as
cheap as Volscians. They are rising, they are rising.

ALL.
In, in, in, in!

[Exeunt.]

SCENE VI. ROME. A PUBLIC PLACE.

[Enter SICINIUS and BRUTUS.]

SICINIUS.
We hear not of him, neither need we fear him;
His remedies are tame i' the present peace
And quietness of the people, which before
Were in wild hurry. Here do make his friends
Blush that the world goes well; who rather had,
Though they themselves did suffer by't, behold
Dissentious numbers pestering streets than see
Our tradesmen singing in their shops, and going
About their functions friendly.

BRUTUS.
We stood to't in good time.—Is this Menenius?

SICINIUS.
'Tis he, 'tis he. O, he is grown most kind
Of late.

[Enter MENENIUS]

BRUTUS.
  Hail, sir!

MENENIUS.
  Hail to you both!

SICINIUS.
  Your Coriolanus is not much miss'd
  But with his friends: the commonwealth doth stand;
  And so would do, were he more angry at it.

MENENIUS.
  All's well, and might have been much better if
  He could have temporiz'd.

SICINIUS.
  Where is he, hear you?

MENENIUS.
  Nay, I hear nothing: his mother and his wife
  Hear nothing from him.

[Enter three or four Citizens.]

CITIZENS. The gods preserve you both!

SICINIUS.
  God-den, our neighbours.

BRUTUS.
  God-den to you all, God-den to you all.

FIRST CITIZEN.
  Ourselves, our wives, and children, on our knees,
  Are bound to pray for you both.

SICINIUS.
  Live and thrive!

BRUTUS.
  Farewell, kind neighbours: we wish'd Coriolanus
  Had lov'd you as we did.

CITIZENS.
  Now the gods keep you!

BOTH TRIBUNES.
  Farewell, farewell.

[Exeunt Citizens.]

SICINIUS.
  This is a happier and more comely time
  Than when these fellows ran about the streets
  Crying confusion.

BRUTUS.
  Caius Marcius was
  A worthy officer i' the war; but insolent,
  O'ercome with pride, ambitious past all thinking,
  Self-loving,—

SICINIUS.
  And affecting one sole throne,
  Without assistance.

MENENIUS.
  I think not so.

SICINIUS.
  We should by this, to all our lamentation,
  If he had gone forth consul, found it so.

BRUTUS.
  The gods have well prevented it, and Rome
  Sits safe and still without him.

[Enter an AEDILE.]

AEDILE.
  Worthy tribunes,
  There is a slave, whom we have put in prison,
  Reports,—the Volsces with several powers
  Are enter'd in the Roman territories,
  And with the deepest malice of the war
  Destroy what lies before 'em.

MENENIUS.
  'Tis Aufidius,
  Who, hearing of our Marcius' banishment,
  Thrusts forth his horns again into the world;

Which were inshell'd when Marcius stood for Rome,
And durst not once peep out.

SICINIUS.
  Come, what talk you of Marcius?

BRUTUS.
  Go see this rumourer whipp'd.—It cannot be
  The Volsces dare break with us.

MENENIUS.
  Cannot be!
  We have record that very well it can;
  And three examples of the like hath been
  Within my age. But reason with the fellow,
  Before you punish him, where he heard this;
  Lest you shall chance to whip your information
  And beat the messenger who bids beware
  Of what is to be dreaded.

SICINIUS.
  Tell not me:
  I know this cannot be.

BRUTUS.
  Not possible.

[Enter A MESSENGER.]

MESSENGER.
  The nobles in great earnestness are going
  All to the senate-house: some news is come
  That turns their countenances.

SICINIUS.
  'Tis this slave,—
  Go whip him fore the people's eyes:—his raising;
  Nothing but his report.

MESSENGER.
  Yes, worthy sir,
  The slave's report is seconded, and more,
  More fearful, is deliver'd.

SICINIUS.
  What more fearful?

MESSENGER.
  It is spoke freely out of many mouths,—
  How probable I do not know,—that Marcius,
  Join'd with Aufidius, leads a power 'gainst Rome,
  And vows revenge as spacious as between
  The young'st and oldest thing.

SICINIUS.
  This is most likely!

BRUTUS.
  Rais'd only, that the weaker sort may wish
  Good Marcius home again.

SICINIUS.
  The very trick on 't.

MENENIUS.
  This is unlikely:
  He and Aufidius can no more atone
  Than violentest contrariety.

[Enter a second MESSENGER.]

SECOND MESSENGER.
  You are sent for to the senate:
  A fearful army, led by Caius Marcius
  Associated with Aufidius, rages
  Upon our territories; and have already
  O'erborne their way, consum'd with fire and took
  What lay before them.

[Enter COMINIUS.]

COMINIUS.
  O, you have made good work!

MENENIUS.
  What news? what news?

COMINIUS.
  You have holp to ravish your own daughters, and
  To melt the city leads upon your pates;
  To see your wives dishonour'd to your noses,—

MENENIUS.
  What's the news? what's the news?

COMINIUS.
  Your temples burned in their cement; and
  Your franchises, whereon you stood, confin'd
  Into an auger's bore.

MENENIUS.
  Pray now, your news?—
  You have made fair work, I fear me.—Pray, your news.
  If Marcius should be join'd wi' the Volscians,—

COMINIUS.
  If!
  He is their god: he leads them like a thing
  Made by some other deity than nature,
  That shapes man better; and they follow him,
  Against us brats, with no less confidence
  Than boys pursuing summer butterflies,
  Or butchers killing flies.

MENENIUS.
  You have made good work,
  You and your apron men; you that stood so much
  Upon the voice of occupation and
  The breath of garlic-eaters!

COMINIUS.
  He'll shake
  Your Rome about your ears.

MENENIUS.
  As Hercules
  Did shake down mellow fruit.—You have made fair work!

BRUTUS.
  But is this true, sir?

COMINIUS.
Ay; and you'll look pale
Before you find it other. All the regions
Do smilingly revolt; and who resists
Are mock'd for valiant ignorance,
And perish constant fools. Who is't can blame him?
Your enemies and his find something in him.

MENENIUS.
We are all undone unless
The noble man have mercy.

COMINIUS.
Who shall ask it?
The tribunes cannot do't for shame; the people
Deserve such pity of him as the wolf
Does of the shepherds: for his best friends, if they
Should say 'Be good to Rome,' they charg'd him even
As those should do that had deserv'd his hate,
And therein show'd like enemies.

MENENIUS.
'Tis true:
If he were putting to my house the brand
That should consume it, I have not the face
To say 'Beseech you, cease.'—You have made fair hands,
You and your crafts! You have crafted fair!

COMINIUS.
You have brought
A trembling upon Rome, such as was never
So incapable of help.

BOTH TRIBUNES.
Say not, we brought it.

MENENIUS.
How! Was it we? we lov'd him, but, like beasts,
And cowardly nobles, gave way unto your clusters,
Who did hoot him out o' the city.

COMINIUS.
But I fear
They'll roar him in again. Tullus Aufidius,

The second name of men, obeys his points
As if he were his officer:—desperation
Is all the policy, strength, and defence,
That Rome can make against them.

[Enter a troop of citizens.]

MENENIUS.
Here comes the clusters.—
And is Aufidius with him?—You are they
That made the air unwholesome, when you cast
Your stinking greasy caps in hooting at
Coriolanus' exile. Now he's coming;
And not a hair upon a soldier's head
Which will not prove a whip: as many coxcombs
As you threw caps up will he tumble down,
And pay you for your voices. 'Tis no matter;
If he could burn us all into one coal
We have deserv'd it.

CITIZENS.
Faith, we hear fearful news.

FIRST CITIZEN.
For mine own part,
When I said banish him, I said 'twas pity.

SECOND CITIZEN.
And so did I.

THIRD CITIZEN. And so did I; and, to say the truth, so
did very many of us. That we did, we did for the best; and
though we willingly consented to his banishment, yet it
was against our will.

COMINIUS.
You are goodly things, you voices!

MENENIUS.
You have made
Good work, you and your cry!—Shall's to the Capitol?

COMINIUS.
O, ay; what else?

William Shakespeare

[Exeunt COMINIUS and MENENIUS.]

SICINIUS.
Go, masters, get you home; be not dismay'd;
These are a side that would be glad to have
This true which they so seem to fear. Go home,
And show no sign of fear.

FIRST CITIZEN. The gods be good to us!—Come, masters, let's home. I ever said we were i' the wrong when we
banished him.

SECOND CITIZEN.
So did we all. But come, let's home.

[Exeunt Citizens.]

BRUTUS.
I do not like this news.

SICINIUS.
Nor I.

BRUTUS.
Let's to the Capitol:—would half my wealth
Would buy this for a lie!

SICINIUS.
Pray let's go.

[Exeunt.]

SCENE VII. A CAMP AT A SHORT DISTANCE FROM ROME.

[Enter AUFIDIUS and his LIEUTENANT.]

AUFIDIUS.
Do they still fly to the Roman?

LIEUTENANT.
I do not know what witchcraft's in him, but
Your soldiers use him as the grace 'fore meat,
Their talk at table, and their thanks at end;
And you are darken'd in this action, sir,
Even by your own.

AUFIDIUS.

I cannot help it now,
Unless by using means, I lame the foot
Of our design. He bears himself more proudlier,
Even to my person, than I thought he would
When first I did embrace him: yet his nature
In that's no changeling; and I must excuse
What cannot be amended.

LIEUTENANT.

Yet I wish, sir,—
I mean, for your particular,—you had not
Join'd in commission with him; but either
Had borne the action of yourself, or else
To him had left it solely.

AUFIDIUS.

I understand thee well; and be thou sure,
When he shall come to his account, he knows not
What I can urge against him. Although it seems,
And so he thinks, and is no less apparent
To the vulgar eye, that he bears all things fairly,
And shows good husbandry for the Volscian state,
Fights dragon-like, and does achieve as soon
As draw his sword: yet he hath left undone
That which shall break his neck or hazard mine
Whene'er we come to our account.

LIEUTENANT.

Sir, I beseech you, think you he'll carry Rome?

AUFIDIUS.

All places yield to him ere he sits down;
And the nobility of Rome are his;
The senators and patricians love him too:
The tribunes are no soldiers; and their people
Will be as rash in the repeal as hasty
To expel him thence. I think he'll be to Rome
As is the osprey to the fish, who takes it
By sovereignty of nature. First he was
A noble servant to them; but he could not
Carry his honours even: whether 'twas pride,
Which out of daily fortune ever taints

The happy man; whether defect of judgment,
To fail in the disposing of those chances
Which he was lord of; or whether nature,
Not to be other than one thing, not moving
From the casque to the cushion, but commanding peace
Even with the same austerity and garb
As he controll'd the war; but one of these,—
As he hath spices of them all, not all,
For I dare so far free him,—made him fear'd,
So hated, and so banish'd: but he has a merit
To choke it in the utterance. So our virtues
Lie in the interpretation of the time:
And power, unto itself most commendable,
Hath not a tomb so evident as a cheer
To extol what it hath done.
One fire drives out one fire; one nail, one nail;
Rights by rights falter, strengths by strengths do fail.
Come, let's away. When, Caius, Rome is thine,
Thou art poor'st of all; then shortly art thou mine.

[Exeunt.]

ACT V.

SCENE I. ROME. A PUBLIC PLACE

[Enter MENENIUS, COMINIUS, SICINIUS and BRUTUS, and others.]

MENENIUS.
No, I'll not go: you hear what he hath said
Which was sometime his general; who lov'd him
In a most dear particular. He call'd me father:
But what o' that? Go, you that banish'd him;
A mile before his tent fall down, and knee
The way into his mercy: nay, if he coy'd
To hear Cominius speak, I'll keep at home.

COMINIUS.
He would not seem to know me.

MENENIUS.
Do you hear?

COMINIUS.
Yet one time he did call me by my name:
I urged our old acquaintance, and the drops
That we have bled together. Coriolanus
He would not answer to: forbad all names;
He was a kind of nothing, titleless,
Till he had forg'd himself a name i' the fire
Of burning Rome.

MENENIUS.
Why, so!—you have made good work!
A pair of tribunes that have rack'd for Rome,
To make coals cheap,—a noble memory!

COMINIUS.
I minded him how royal 'twas to pardon
When it was less expected: he replied,
It was a bare petition of a state
To one whom they had punish'd.

MENENIUS.
  Very well:
  Could he say less?

COMINIUS.
  I offer'd to awaken his regard
  For's private friends: his answer to me was,
  He could not stay to pick them in a pile
  Of noisome musty chaff: he said 'twas folly,
  For one poor grain or two, to leave unburnt
  And still to nose the offence.

MENENIUS.
  For one poor grain
  Or two! I am one of those; his mother, wife,
  His child, and this brave fellow too- we are the grains:
  You are the musty chaff; and you are smelt
  Above the moon: we must be burnt for you.

SICINIUS.
  Nay, pray be patient: if you refuse your aid
  In this so never-needed help, yet do not
  Upbraid's with our distress. But, sure, if you
  Would be your country's pleader, your good tongue,
  More than the instant army we can make,
  Might stop our countryman.

MENENIUS.
  No; I'll not meddle.

SICINIUS.
  Pray you, go to him.

MENENIUS.
  What should I do?

BRUTUS.
  Only make trial what your love can do
  For Rome, towards Marcius.

MENENIUS.
  Well, and say that Marcius
  Return me, as Cominius is return'd,
  Unheard; what then?

But as a discontented friend, grief-shot
With his unkindness? Say't be so?

SICINIUS.
  Yet your good-will
  Must have that thanks from Rome, after the measure
  As you intended well.

MENENIUS.
  I'll undertake't;
  I think he'll hear me. Yet to bite his lip
  And hum at good Cominius much unhearts me.
  He was not taken well: he had not din'd;
  The veins unfill'd, our blood is cold, and then
  We pout upon the morning, are unapt
  To give or to forgive; but when we have stuff'd
  These pipes and these conveyances of our blood
  With wine and feeding, we have suppler souls
  Than in our priest-like fasts. Therefore I'll watch him
  Till he be dieted to my request,
  And then I'll set upon him.

BRUTUS.
  You know the very road into his kindness
  And cannot lose your way.

MENENIUS.
  Good faith, I'll prove him,
  Speed how it will. I shall ere long have knowledge
  Of my success.

[Exit.]

COMINIUS.
  He'll never hear him.

SICINIUS.
  Not?

COMINIUS.
  I tell you he does sit in gold, his eye
  Red as 'twould burn Rome: and his injury
  The gaoler to his pity. I kneel'd before him;
  'Twas very faintly he said 'Rise'; dismissed me

Thus, with his speechless hand: what he would do,
He sent in writing after me; what he would not,
Bound with an oath to yield to his conditions:
So that all hope is vain,
Unless his noble mother and his wife;
Who, as I hear, mean to solicit him
For mercy to his country. Therefore, let's hence,
And with our fair entreaties haste them on.

[Exeunt.]

SCENE II. AN ADVANCED POST OF THE VOLSCIAN CAMP BEFORE ROME. THE GUARDS AT THEIR STATION.

[Enter to them MENENIUS.]

FIRST GUARD.
  Stay: whence are you?

SECOND GUARD.
  Stand, and go back.

MENENIUS.
  You guard like men; 'tis well: but, by your leave,
  I am an officer of state, and come
  To speak with Coriolanus.

FIRST GUARD.
  From whence?

MENENIUS.
  From Rome.

FIRST GUARD.
  You may not pass; you must return: our general
  Will no more hear from thence.

SECOND GUARD.
  You'll see your Rome embrac'd with fire before
  You'll speak with Coriolanus.

MENENIUS.
  Good my friends,
  If you have heard your general talk of Rome
  And of his friends there, it is lots to blanks
  My name hath touch'd your ears: it is Menenius.

FIRST GUARD.
  Be it so; go back: the virtue of your name
  Is not here passable.

MENENIUS.
  I tell thee, fellow,
  Thy general is my lover: I have been
  The book of his good acts, whence men have read
  His fame unparallel'd, haply amplified;
  For I have ever verified my friends,—
  Of whom he's chief,—with all the size that verity
  Would without lapsing suffer: nay, sometimes,
  Like to a bowl upon a subtle ground,
  I have tumbled past the throw: and in his praise
  Have almost stamp'd the leasing: therefore, fellow,
  I must have leave to pass.

FIRST GUARD. Faith, sir, if you had told as many lies in his
  behalf as you have uttered words in your own, you should
  not pass here: no, though it were as virtuous to lie as to live
  chastely. Therefore, go back.

MENENIUS. Pr'ythee, fellow, remember my name is Menenius, always factionary on the party of your general.

SECOND GUARD. Howsoever you have been his liar,—as
  you say you have, I am one that, telling true under him,
  must say you cannot pass. Therefore go back.

MENENIUS. Has he dined, canst thou tell? For I would not
  speak with him till after dinner.

FIRST GUARD.
  You are a Roman, are you?

MENENIUS.
  I am as thy general is.

FIRST GUARD. Then you should hate Rome, as he does.
  Can you, when you have pushed out your gates the very
  defender of them, and in a violent popular ignorance,
  given your enemy your shield, think to front his revenges
  with the easy groans of old women, the virginal palms of
  your daughters, or with the palsied intercession of such a

decayed dotant as you seem to be? Can you think to blow out the intended fire your city is ready to flame in, with such weak breath as this? No, you are deceived; therefore back to Rome, and prepare for your execution: you are condemned; our general has sworn you out of reprieve and pardon.

MENENIUS. Sirrah, if thy captain knew I were here he would use me with estimation.

SECOND GUARD.
  Come, my captain knows you not.

MENENIUS.
  I mean thy general.

FIRST GUARD. My general cares not for you. Back, I say; go, lest I let forth your half pint of blood;—back; that's the utmost of your having:—back.

MENENIUS.
  Nay, but fellow, fellow,—

[Enter CORIOLANUS with AUFIDIUS.]

CORIOLANUS.
  What's the matter?

MENENIUS. Now, you companion, I'll say an errand for you; you shall know now that I am in estimation; you shall perceive that a jack guardant cannot office me from my son Coriolanus: guess but by my entertainment with him if thou standest not i' the state of hanging, or of some death more long in spectatorship and crueller in suffering; behold now presently, and swoon for what's to come upon thee.— The glorious gods sit in hourly synod about thy particular prosperity, and love thee no worse than thy old father Menenius does! O my son! my son! thou art preparing fire for us; look thee, here's water to quench it. I was hardly moved to come to thee; but being assured none but myself could move thee, I have been blown out of your gates with sighs; and conjure thee to pardon Rome and thy petitionary countrymen. The good gods assuage thy wrath, and turn the dregs of it upon this varlet here; this, who, like a block, hath denied my access to thee.

CORIOLANUS.
  Away!

MENENIUS.
  How! away!

CORIOLANUS.
  Wife, mother, child, I know not. My affairs
  Are servanted to others: though I owe
  My revenge properly, my remission lies
  In Volscian breasts. That we have been familiar,
  Ingrate forgetfulness shall poison, rather
  Than pity note how much.—Therefore be gone.
  Mine ears against your suits are stronger than
  Your gates against my force. Yet, for I lov'd thee,
  Take this along; I writ it for thy sake,

[Gives a letter.]

And would have sent it. Another word, Menenius,
  I will not hear thee speak.—This man, Aufidius,
  Was my beloved in Rome: yet thou behold'st!

AUFIDIUS.
  You keep a constant temper.

[Exeunt CORIOLANUS and AUFIDIUS.]

FIRST GUARD.
  Now, sir, is your name Menenius?

SECOND GUARD. 'Tis a spell, you see, of much power:
  you know the way home again.

FIRST GUARD.
  Do you hear how we are shent for keeping your greatness
  back?

SECOND GUARD.
  What cause, do you think, I have to swoon?

MENENIUS. I neither care for the world nor your general;
  for such things as you, I can scarce think there's any, y'are
  so slight. He that hath a will to die by himself fears it not
  from another. Let your general do his worst. For you, be

that you are, long; and your misery increase with your age!
I say to you, as I was said to, away!

[Exit.]

FIRST GUARD.
  A noble fellow, I warrant him.

SECOND GUARD. The worthy fellow is our general: he is
  the rock, the oak not to be wind-shaken.

[Exeunt.]

SCENE III. THE TENT OF CORIOLANUS.

[Enter CORIOLANUS, AUFIDIUS, and others.]

CORIOLANUS.
  We will before the walls of Rome to-morrow
  Set down our host.—My partner in this action,
  You must report to the Volscian lords how plainly
  I have borne this business.

AUFIDIUS.
  Only their ends
  You have respected; stopped your ears against
  The general suit of Rome; never admitted
  A private whisper, no, not with such friends
  That thought them sure of you.

CORIOLANUS.
  This last old man,
  Whom with crack'd heart I have sent to Rome,
  Lov'd me above the measure of a father;
  Nay, godded me indeed. Their latest refuge
  Was to send him; for whose old love I have,—
  Though I show'd sourly to him,—once more offer'd
  The first conditions, which they did refuse,
  And cannot now accept, to grace him only,
  That thought he could do more, a very little
  I have yielded to: fresh embassies and suits,
  Nor from the state nor private friends, hereafter
  Will I lend ear to.—

[Shout within.]

Ha! what shout is this?
  Shall I be tempted to infringe my vow
  In the same time 'tis made? I will not.

[Enter, in mourning habits, VIRGILIA, VOLUMNIA, leading YOUNG
  MARCIUS, VALERIA, and attendants.]

My wife comes foremost; then the honour'd mould
  Wherein this trunk was fram'd, and in her hand
  The grandchild to her blood. But, out, affection!
  All bond and privilege of nature, break!
  Let it be virtuous to be obstinate.—
  What is that curt'sy worth? or those doves' eyes,
  Which can make gods forsworn?—I melt, and am not
  Of stronger earth than others.—My mother bows,
  As if Olympus to a molehill should
  In supplication nod: and my young boy
  Hath an aspect of intercession which
  Great nature cries "Deny not.'—Let the Volsces
  Plough Rome and harrow Italy: I'll never
  Be such a gosling to obey instinct; but stand,
  As if a man were author of himself,
  And knew no other kin.

VIRGILIA.
  My lord and husband!

CORIOLANUS.
  These eyes are not the same I wore in Rome.

VIRGILIA.
  The sorrow that delivers us thus chang'd
  Makes you think so.

CORIOLANUS.
  Like a dull actor now,
  I have forgot my part and I am out,
  Even to a full disgrace. Best of my flesh,
  Forgive my tyranny; but do not say,
  For that, 'Forgive our Romans.'—O, a kiss
  Long as my exile, sweet as my revenge;
  Now, by the jealous queen of heaven, that kiss
  I carried from thee, dear; and my true lip

Hath virgin'd it e'er since.—You gods! I prate,
And the most noble mother of the world
Leave unsaluted: sink, my knee, i' the earth;

[Kneels.]

Of thy deep duty more impression show
  Than that of common sons.

VOLUMNIA.
  O, stand up bless'd!
  Whilst, with no softer cushion than the flint,
  I kneel before thee; and unproperly
  Show duty, as mistaken all this while
  Between the child and parent.

[Kneels.]

CORIOLANUS.
  What is this?
  Your knees to me? to your corrected son?
  Then let the pebbles on the hungry beach
  Fillip the stars; then let the mutinous winds
  Strike the proud cedars 'gainst the fiery sun,;
  Murdering impossibility, to make
  What cannot be, slight work.

VOLUMNIA.
  Thou art my warrior;
  I holp to frame thee. Do you know this lady?

CORIOLANUS.
  The noble sister of Publicola,
  The moon of Rome; chaste as the icicle
  That's curded by the frost from purest snow,
  And hangs on Dian's temple:—dear Valeria!

VOLUMNIA.
  This is a poor epitome of yours,
  Which, by the interpretation of full time,
  May show like all yourself.

CORIOLANUS.
  The god of soldiers,

With the consent of supreme Jove, inform
Thy thoughts with nobleness; that thou mayst prove
To shame unvulnerable, and stick i' the wars
Like a great sea-mark, standing every flaw,
And saving those that eye thee!

VOLUMNIA.
  Your knee, sirrah.

CORIOLANUS.
  That's my brave boy.

VOLUMNIA.
  Even he, your wife, this lady, and myself,
  Are suitors to you.

CORIOLANUS.
  I beseech you, peace:
  Or, if you'd ask, remember this before,—
  The thing I have forsworn to grant may never
  Be held by you denials. Do not bid me
  Dismiss my soldiers, or capitulate
  Again with Rome's mechanics.—Tell me not
  Wherein I seem unnatural: desire not
  To allay my rages and revenges with
  Your colder reasons.

VOLUMNIA.
  O, no more, no more!
  You have said you will not grant us anything;
  For we have nothing else to ask but that
  Which you deny already: yet we will ask;
  That, if you fail in our request, the blame
  May hang upon your hardness; therefore hear us.

CORIOLANUS.
  Aufidius, and you Volsces, mark: for we'll
  Hear nought from Rome in private.—Your request?

VOLUMNIA.
  Should we be silent and not speak, our raiment
  And state of bodies would bewray what life
  We have led since thy exile. Think with thyself,
  How more unfortunate than all living women

Are we come hither: since that thy sight, which should
Make our eyes flow with joy, hearts dance with comforts,
Constrains them weep, and shake with fear and sorrow;
Making the mother, wife, and child, to see
The son, the husband, and the father, tearing
His country's bowels out. And to poor we,
Thine enmity's most capital: thou barr'st us
Our prayers to the gods, which is a comfort
That all but we enjoy; for how can we,
Alas, how can we for our country pray,
Whereto we are bound,—together with thy victory,
Whereto we are bound? alack, or we must lose
The country, our dear nurse, or else thy person,
Our comfort in the country. We must find
An evident calamity, though we had
Our wish, which side should win; for either thou
Must, as a foreign recreant, be led
With manacles through our streets, or else
Triumphantly tread on thy country's ruin,
And bear the palm for having bravely shed
Thy wife and children's blood. For myself, son,
I purpose not to wait on fortune till
These wars determine: if I can not persuade thee
Rather to show a noble grace to both parts
Than seek the end of one, thou shalt no sooner
March to assault thy country than to tread,—
Trust to't, thou shalt not,—on thy mother's womb
That brought thee to this world.

VIRGILIA.
　Ay, and mine,
　That brought you forth this boy, to keep your name
　Living to time.

BOY.
　'A shall not tread on me;
　I'll run away till I am bigger; but then I'll fight.

CORIOLANUS.
　Not of a woman's tenderness to be,
　Requires nor child nor woman's face to see.
　I have sat too long.

[Rising.]

VOLUMNIA.
  Nay, go not from us thus.
  If it were so that our request did tend
  To save the Romans, thereby to destroy
  The Volsces whom you serve, you might condemn us,
  As poisonous of your honour: no; our suit
  Is that you reconcile them: while the Volsces
  May say 'This mercy we have show'd,' the Romans
  'This we receiv'd,' and each in either side
  Give the all-hail to thee, and cry, 'Be bless'd
  For making up this peace!' Thou know'st, great son,
  The end of war's uncertain; but this certain,
  That, if thou conquer Rome, the benefit
  Which thou shalt thereby reap is such a name
  Whose repetition will be dogg'd with curses;
  Whose chronicle thus writ:—'The man was noble,
  But with his last attempt he wip'd it out;
  Destroy'd his country, and his name remains
  To the ensuing age abhorr'd.' Speak to me, son:
  Thou hast affected the fine strains of honour,
  To imitate the graces of the gods,
  To tear with thunder the wide cheeks o' the air,
  And yet to charge thy sulphur with a bolt
  That should but rive an oak. Why dost not speak?
  Think'st thou it honourable for a noble man
  Still to remember wrongs?—Daughter, speak you:
  He cares not for your weeping.—Speak thou, boy:
  Perhaps thy childishness will move him more
  Than can our reasons.—There's no man in the world
  More bound to's mother; yet here he lets me prate
  Like one i' the stocks. Thou hast never in thy life
  Show'd thy dear mother any courtesy;
  When she,—poor hen,—fond of no second brood,
  Has cluck'd thee to the wars, and safely home,
  Loaden with honour. Say my request's unjust,
  And spurn me back: but if it be not so,
  Thou art not honest; and the gods will plague thee,
  That thou restrain'st from me the duty which
  To a mother's part belongs.—He turns away:
  Down, ladies: let us shame him with our knees.

To his surname Coriolanus 'longs more pride
Than pity to our prayers. Down: an end;
This is the last.—So we will home to Rome,
And die among our neighbours.—Nay, behold's:
This boy, that cannot tell what he would have
But kneels and holds up hands for fellowship,
Does reason our petition with more strength
Than thou hast to deny't.—Come, let us go:
This fellow had a Volscian to his mother;
His wife is in Corioli, and his child
Like him by chance.—Yet give us our despatch:
I am hush'd until our city be afire,
And then I'll speak a little.

CORIOLANUS.
[After holding VOLUMNIA by the hands, in silence.]
O mother, mother!
What have you done? Behold, the heavens do ope,
The gods look down, and this unnatural scene
They laugh at. O my mother, mother! O!
You have won a happy victory to Rome;
But for your son,—believe it, O, believe it,
Most dangerously you have with him prevail'd,
If not most mortal to him. But let it come.—
Aufidius, though I cannot make true wars,
I'll frame convenient peace. Now, good Aufidius,
Were you in my stead, would you have heard
A mother less? or granted less, Aufidius?

AUFIDIUS.
I was mov'd withal.

CORIOLANUS.
I dare be sworn you were:
And, sir, it is no little thing to make
Mine eyes to sweat compassion. But, good sir,
What peace you'll make, advise me: for my part,
I'll not to Rome, I'll back with you; and, pray you
Stand to me in this cause.—O mother! wife!

AUFIDIUS.
[Aside.] I am glad thou hast set thy mercy and thy honour
At difference in thee; out of that I'll work
Myself a former fortune.

[The Ladies make signs to CORIOLANUS.]

CORIOLANUS.
  [To VOLUMNIA, VIRGILIA, &c.] Ay, by and by;
  But we'll drink together; and you shall bear
  A better witness back than words, which we,
  On like conditions, will have counter-seal'd.
  Come, enter with us. Ladies, you deserve
  To have a temple built you: all the swords
  In Italy, and her confederate arms,
  Could not have made this peace.

[Exeunt.]

SCENE IV. ROME. A PUBLIC PLACE.

[Enter MENENIUS and SICINIUS.]

MENENIUS.
  See you yond coign o' the Capitol,—yond corner-stone?

SICINIUS.
  Why, what of that?

MENENIUS. If it be possible for you to displace it with your
  little finger, there is some hope the ladies of Rome, especially his mother, may prevail with him. But I say there
  is no hope in't: our throats are sentenced, and stay upon
  execution.

SICINIUS. Is't possible that so short a time can alter the
  condition of a man?

MENENIUS. There is differency between a grub and a
  butterfly; yet your butterfly was a grub. This Marcius is
  grown from man to dragon; he has wings; he's more than a
  creeping thing.

SICINIUS.
  He loved his mother dearly.

MENENIUS. So did he me: and he no more remembers his
  mother now than an eight-year-old horse. The tartness of
  his face sours ripe grapes: when he walks, he moves like
  an engine, and the ground shrinks before his treading: he is

able to pierce a corslet with his eye, talks like a knell, and his hum is a battery. He sits in his state as a thing made for Alexander. What he bids be done is finished with his bidding. He wants nothing of a god but eternity, and a heaven to throne in.

SICINIUS.
Yes, mercy, if you report him truly.

MENENIUS. I paint him in the character. Mark what mercy his mother shall bring from him. There is no more mercy in him than there is milk in a male tiger; that shall our poor city find: and all this is 'long of you.

SICINIUS.
The gods be good unto us!

MENENIUS. No, in such a case the gods will not be good unto us. When we banished him we respected not them; and, he returning to break our necks, they respect not us.

[Enter a MESSENGER

MESSENGER.
Sir, if you'd save your life, fly to your house:
The plebeians have got your fellow-tribune
And hale him up and down; all swearing, if
The Roman ladies bring not comfort home
They'll give him death by inches.

[Enter a second MESSENGER.]

SICINIUS.
What's the news?

SECOND MESSENGER.
Good news, good news;—the ladies have prevail'd,
The Volscians are dislodg'd, and Marcius gone:
A merrier day did never yet greet Rome,
No, not the expulsion of the Tarquins.

SICINIUS.
Friend,
Art thou certain this is true? is't most certain?

SECOND MESSENGER.
　As certain as I know the sun is fire:
　Where have you lurk'd, that you make doubt of it?
　Ne'er through an arch so hurried the blown tide
　As the recomforted through the gates. Why, hark you!

[Trumpets and hautboys sounded, drums beaten, aand shout-
　ing within.]

The trumpets, sackbuts, psalteries, and fifes,
　Tabors and cymbals, and the shouting Romans,
　Make the sun dance. Hark you!

[Shouting within.]

MENENIUS.
　This is good news.
　I will go meet the ladies. This Volumnia
　Is worth of consuls, senators, patricians,
　A city full: of tribunes such as you,
　A sea and land full. You have pray'd well to-day:
　This morning for ten thousand of your throats
　Ied not have given a doit. Hark, how they joy!

[Shouting and music.]

SICINIUS.
　First, the gods bless you for your tidings; next,
　Accept my thankfulness.

SECOND MESSENGER.
　Sir, we have all
　Great cause to give great thanks.

SICINIUS.
　They are near the city?

MESSENGER.
　Almost at point to enter.

SICINIUS.
　We'll meet them,
　And help the joy.

[Exeunt.]

SCENE V. ROME. A STREET NEAR THE GATE.

[Enter VOLUMNIA, VIRGILIA, VALERIA, &c., accompanied by Senators,
  Patricians, and Citizens.]

FIRST SENATOR.
  Behold our patroness, the life of Rome!
  Call all your tribes together, praise the gods,
  And make triumphant fires; strew flowers before them:
  Unshout the noise that banish'd Marcius,
  Repeal him with the welcome of his mother;
  Cry, 'Welcome, ladies, welcome!'—

ALL.
  Welcome, ladies,
  Welcome!

[Exeunt.]

SCENE VI. ANTIUM. A PUBLIC PLACE.

[Enter TULLUS AUFIDIUS, with attendants.]

AUFIDIUS.
  Go tell the lords o' the city I am here:
  Deliver them this paper; having read it,
  Bid them repair to the market-place: where I,
  Even in theirs and in the commons' ears,
  Will vouch the truth of it. Him I accuse
  The city ports by this hath enter'd and
  Intends t' appear before the people, hoping
  To purge himself with words: despatch.

[Exeunt attendants.]

[Enter three or four CONSPIRATORS of AUFIDIUS' fac-
  tion.]

Most welcome!

FIRST CONSPIRATOR.
  How is it with our general?

AUFIDIUS.
  Even so
  As with a man by his own alms empoison'd,
  And with his charity slain.

SECOND CONSPIRATOR.
  Most noble sir,
  If you do hold the same intent wherein
  You wish'd us parties, we'll deliver you
  Of your great danger.

AUFIDIUS.
  Sir, I cannot tell:
  We must proceed as we do find the people.

THIRD CONSPIRATOR.
  The people will remain uncertain whilst
  'Twixt you there's difference: but the fall of either
  Makes the survivor heir of all.

AUFIDIUS.
  I know it;
  And my pretext to strike at him admits
  A good construction. I rais'd him, and I pawn'd
  Mine honour for his truth: who being so heighten'd,
  He water'd his new plants with dews of flattery,
  Seducing so my friends; and to this end
  He bow'd his nature, never known before
  But to be rough, unswayable, and free.

THIRD CONSPIRATOR.
  Sir, his stoutness
  When he did stand for consul, which he lost
  By lack of stooping,—

AUFIDIUS.
  That I would have spoken of:
  Being banish'd for't, he came unto my hearth;
  Presented to my knife his throat: I took him;
  Made him joint-servant with me; gave him way
  In all his own desires; nay, let him choose
  Out of my files, his projects to accomplish,
  My best and freshest men; serv'd his designments
  In mine own person; holp to reap the fame

Which he made all his; and took some pride
To do myself this wrong: till, at the last,
I seem'd his follower, not partner; and
He wag'd me with his countenance as if
I had been mercenary.

FIRST CONSPIRATOR.
  So he did, my lord:
  The army marvell'd at it; and, in the last,
  When he had carried Rome, and that we look'd
  For no less spoil than glory,—

AUFIDIUS.
  There was it;—
  For which my sinews shall be stretch'd upon him.
  At a few drops of women's rheum, which are
  As cheap as lies, he sold the blood and labour
  Of our great action: therefore shall he die,
  And I'll renew me in his fall. But, hark!

[Drums and trumpets sound, with great shouts of the people.]

FIRST CONSPIRATOR.
  Your native town you enter'd like a post,
  And had no welcomes home; but he returns
  Splitting the air with noise.

SECOND CONSPIRATOR.
  And patient fools,
  Whose children he hath slain, their base throats tear
  With giving him glory.

THIRD CONSPIRATOR.
  Therefore, at your vantage,
  Ere he express himself or move the people
  With what he would say, let him feel your sword,
  Which we will second. When he lies along,
  After your way his tale pronounc'd shall bury
  His reasons with his body.

AUFIDIUS.
  Say no more:
  Here come the lords.

[Enter the LORDS of the city.]

LORDS.
  You are most welcome home.

AUFIDIUS.
  I have not deserv'd it.
  But, worthy lords, have you with heed perus'd
  What I have written to you?

LORDS.
  We have.

FIRST LORD.
  And grieve to hear't.
  What faults he made before the last, I think
  Might have found easy fines: but there to end
  Where he was to begin, and give away
  The benefit of our levies, answering us
  With our own charge: making a treaty where
  There was a yielding.—This admits no excuse.

AUFIDIUS.
  He approaches: you shall hear him.

[Enter CORIOLANUS, with drum and colours; a crowd of
  Citizens with him.]

CORIOLANUS.
  Hail, lords! I am return'd your soldier;
  No more infected with my country's love
  Than when I parted hence, but still subsisting
  Under your great command. You are to know
  That prosperously I have attempted, and
  With bloody passage led your wars even to
  The gates of Rome. Our spoils we have brought home
  Do more than counterpoise a full third part
  The charges of the action. We have made peace
  With no less honour to the Antiates
  Than shame to the Romans: and we here deliver,
  Subscribed by the consuls and patricians,
  Together with the seal o' the senate, what
  We have compounded on.

AUFIDIUS.
  Read it not, noble lords;
  But tell the traitor, in the highest degree
  He hath abus'd your powers.

CORIOLANUS.
  Traitor!—How now?

AUFIDIUS.
  Ay, traitor, Marcius.

CORIOLANUS.
  Marcius!

AUFIDIUS.
  Ay, Marcius, Caius Marcius! Dost thou think
  I'll grace thee with that robbery, thy stol'n name
  Coriolanus, in Corioli?—
  You lords and heads o' the state, perfidiously
  He has betray'd your business, and given up,
  For certain drops of salt, your city Rome,—
  I say your city,—to his wife and mother;
  Breaking his oath and resolution, like
  A twist of rotten silk; never admitting
  Counsel o' the war; but at his nurse's tears
  He whin'd and roar'd away your victory;
  That pages blush'd at him, and men of heart
  Look'd wondering each at others.

CORIOLANUS.
  Hear'st thou, Mars?

AUFIDIUS.
  Name not the god, thou boy of tears,—

CORIOLANUS.
  Ha!

AUFIDIUS.
  No more.

CORIOLANUS.
  Measureless liar, thou hast made my heart
  Too great for what contains it. Boy! O slave!—

Pardon me, lords, 'tis the first time that ever
I was forc'd to scold. Your judgments, my grave lords,
Must give this cur the lie: and his own notion,—
Who wears my stripes impress'd upon him; that must bear
My beating to his grave,—shall join to thrust
The lie unto him.

FIRST LORD.
Peace, both, and hear me speak.

CORIOLANUS.
Cut me to pieces, Volsces; men and lads,
Stain all your edges on me.—Boy! False hound!
If you have writ your annals true, 'tis there,
That, like an eagle in a dove-cote, I
Flutter'd your Volscians in Corioli:
Alone I did it.—Boy!

AUFIDIUS.
Why, noble lords,
Will you be put in mind of his blind fortune,
Which was your shame, by this unholy braggart,
'Fore your own eyes and ears?

CONSPIRATORS.
Let him die for't.

CITIZENS. Tear him to pieces, do it presently:—he killed
my son; my daughter; he killed my cousin Marcus; he
killed my father,—

SECOND LORD.
Peace, ho!—no outrage;—peace!
The man is noble, and his fame folds in
This orb o' the earth. His last offences to us
Shall have judicious hearing.—Stand, Aufidius,
And trouble not the peace.

CORIOLANUS.
O that I had him,
With six Aufidiuses, or more, his tribe,
To use my lawful sword!

AUFIDIUS.
  Insolent villain!

CONSPIRATORS.
  Kill, kill, kill, kill, kill him!

[AUFIDIUS and the CONSPIRATORS draw, and kill CORI-
  OLANUS,who falls. AUFIDIUS stands on him.]

LORDS.
  Hold, hold, hold, hold!

AUFIDIUS.
  My noble masters, hear me speak.

FIRST LORD.
  O Tullus,—

SECOND LORD.
  Thou hast done a deed whereat valour will weep.

THIRD LORD.
  Tread not upon him.—Masters all, be quiet;
  Put up your swords.

AUFIDIUS.
  My lords, when you shall know,—as in this rage,
  Provok'd by him, you cannot,—the great danger
  Which this man's life did owe you, you'll rejoice
  That he is thus cut off. Please it your honours
  To call me to your senate, I'll deliver
  Myself your loyal servant, or endure
  Your heaviest censure.

FIRST LORD.
  Bear from hence his body,
  And mourn you for him. Let him be regarded
  As the most noble corse that ever herald
  Did follow to his um.

SECOND LORD.
  His own impatience
  Takes from Aufidius a great part of blame.
  Let's make the best of it.

AUFIDIUS.
My rage is gone;
And I am struck with sorrow.—Take him up:—
Help, three o' the chiefest soldiers; I'll be one.—
Beat thou the drum, that it speak mournfully;
Trail your steel pikes. Though in this city he
Hath widow'd and unchilded many a one,
Which to this hour bewail the injury,
Yet he shall have a noble memory.—
Assist.

[Exeunt, bearing the body of CORIOLANUS. A dead march
sounded.]